COMPUTER SYSTEMS AND WATER RESOURCES

DEVELOPMENTS IN WATER SCIENCE

advisory editor
VEN TE CHOW
Professor of Civil Engineering
Hydrosystems Laboratory
Civil Engineering Building
University of Illinois
Urbana, Ill., U.S.A.

DEVELOPMENTS IN WATER SCIENCE

1

COMPUTER SYSTEMS
and
WATER RESOURCES

by

GEORGE BUGLIARELLO
President, Polytechnic Institute of New York

and

FRED GUNTHER
Research Assistant, University of Illinois at Chicago Circle

ELSEVIER SCIENTIFIC PUBLISHING COMPANY

AMSTERDAM — OXFORD — NEW YORK — 1974

ELSEVIER SCIENTIFIC PUBLISHING COMPANY
335 Jan van Galenstraat
P.O. Box 211, Amsterdam, The Netherlands

AMERICAN ELSEVIER PUBLISHING COMPANY, INC.
52 Vanderbilt Avenue
New York, New York 10017

Library of Congress Card Number: 74-83312

ISBN: 0-444-41259-X

Printed in The Netherlands

PREFACE

We should like to state from the outset what this book is not. It is not a study of water resource systems or of methodologies for the planning, design, and operation of such systems—topics that are treated in a vast body of excellent books, papers, and reports which have appeared in recent years. Rather, the book addresses itself to an area in water resources technology that has received practically no attention in the literature: the description and assessment of the pervasive role that computer systems have come to exert in this field, and are likely to exert in the future. While there are few practitioners or researchers in water resources today who have not used a computer in their work, and derived opinions, preferences, and a feeling for the possible directions of future evolution concerning computer systems, it is fair to say that a systematic and comprehensive discussion of the subject has been lacking. Though this book does not provide such a comprehensive discussion, it does offer a state of the art overview of some of the principal considerations concerning computer systems that the decision-maker and practitioner in water resources can no longer afford to neglect. Since we believe that an historical perspective is important, in several sections of the book we have provided brief sketches of the early use of computers in a number of water resource areas.

The germ of the book was a study carried out for the U.S. Office of Water Resources Research[1], which was subsequently expanded, modified, and brought up to date. The study could not have been accomplished without the expertise of numerous persons. In addition to Robert Cheever who was a participant in the original study, numerous persons have contributed their expertise and advice. Personal communications with M. Abbott, E. Altouney, P. Caruso, P. Combs, A. Cosper, N.H. Crawford, B. Doyle, A.J. Frederick, C. Furgeson, S. Lang, H.L. Longford, L. Manning, R. Myrick, J. Orlob, R.V. Thomann, and D.W. Webber, to name only a few, provided valuable direction and insight into the important, but often subtle problems encountered in the establishment of computer and programming policy. Contributions by Sheri Gunther and Brandy Rommel (Editing), Vivian

---

[1] Bugliarello, G. and Gunther, F.J., *Computers and Water Resources,* U.S. Office of Water Resources Research, 1973.

v

Cardwell (Administration), Myra Martin (Typing), and Edward Daniels (Drafting), in dealing with the practical aspects of generating this document cannot be fully acknowledged.

LIST OF ABBREVIATIONS

A-D	Analog to Digital
ADP	Automatic Data Processing
ADTS	Automated Data and Telecommunications Service
AEC	Atomic Energy Commission
Agriculture	Department of Agriculture
ARIS	Automatic Radio Interrogation System
ARS	Agricultural Research Service
ASCE	American Society of Civil Engineers
ASP	Automatic Synthesis Program
BDC	Bureau of Domestic Commerce
BIA	Bureau of Indian Affairs
BLM	Bureau of Land Management
BM	Bureau of Mines
BOD	Biochemical Oxygen Demand
BOR	Bureau of Outdoor Recreation
BPA	Bonneville Power Administration
BR	Bureau of Reclamation
BRECS	Bureau of Reclamation Engineering Computer Systems
BSYS	Bridge System
Calif	California Department of Water Resources
CDA	Command Data Acquisition
CDC	Control Data Corporation
CE	Corps of Engineers
Census	Bureau of the Census
CG	Coast Guard
Commerce	Department of Commerce
CPU	Central Processing Unit
CRT	Cathode Ray Tube
CSC	Computer Sciences Corporation
D-A	Digital to Analog
DEC	Digital Equipment Corporation
DECUS	Digital Equipment Computer Users Society
Defense	Department of Defense
DO	Dissolved Oxygen
DOT	Department of Transportation

EAI	Electronic Associates, Inc.
ECM	Extended Core Memory
EDP	Electronic Data Processing
EDS	Environmental Data Service
EPA	Environmental Protection Agency
ERL	Environmental Research Laboratories
EROS	Earth Resources Observation Satellite
ERTS	Earth Resources Technology Satellite
FHWA	Federal Highway Administration
FPC	Federal Power Commission
FS	Forest Service
FWPCA	Federal Water Pollution Control Admin.
GE	General Electric
GS	Geological Survey
GSA	General Services Administration
HEC	Hydrologic Engineering Center
HEW	Department of Health, Education and Welfare
HR	Hour
HSP	Hydrocomp Simulation Program
HYDC	Hydrocomp, Inc.
HYDS	Hydroscience, Inc.
HUD	Department of Housing and Urban Development
IAHR	International Association of Hydraulic Research
IBM	International Business Machines
IBWC	International Boundry and Water Commission
ICES	Integrated Civil Engineering System
IJC	International Joint Commission
Ind. Agencies	Independent Agencies
INSIGHT	Interactive System for Investigation by Graphics of Hydrological Trends
Interior	Department of the Interior
I/O	Input/Output
ISD	Information System Design
K	Kilo (1000)
kw	Kilowatt
LCS	Large Capacity Storage
MCAUTO	McDonald Automation
Mega	Mega (10^6)
Min	Minute
Mini	Minicomputer
MIT	Massachusetts Institute of Technology

MS	Master of Science
MSPS	Multi-Spectral Point Scanner
MTBF	Mean Time Between Failures
NASA	National Aeronautics and Space Admin.
NAWDEX	National Water Data Exchange
NCC	National Climatic Center
NFEC	Naval Facilities Engineering Command
NMFS	National Marine Fisheries Service
NOAA	National Oceanographic and Atmospheric Adm.
NODC	National Oceanographic Data Center
Non-Federal	Non-Federal Agencies
NOS	National Ocean Survey
NPS	National Park Service
NWS	National Weather Service
N.Y.	New York Department of Environmental Conservation
ORD	Ohio River Division
OSI	Optimum Systems, Inc.
OSW	Office of Saline Water
OWRR	Office of Water Resources Research
Penn	Pennsylvania Department of Health
PhD	Doctor of Philosophy
PHS	Public Health Service
PL/I	Programming Language 1
POL	Problem-Oriented Language
PROGS	Progress of Ground Settlement
PROM	Programmable Read Only Memory
QLM	Quirk, Lawler & Matusky, Inc.
RAM	Random Access Memory
R&D	Research and Development
RJE	Remote Job Entry
ROM	Read Only Memory
SCS	Soil Conservation Service
Sec	Second
SF&W	Bureau of Sport Fisheries and Wildlife
STAR	String Array
State	Department of State
STORET	Storage and Retrieval
TV	Television
TVA	Tennessee Valley Authority
UNIV	Universities, Colleges, etc.
UNMES	Utah New Mexico Earthwork System

USGS	United States Geological Survey
Va	Virginia
Wash	Washington (D.C.)
WPO	Water Programs Office
WRC	Water Resources Council
WRD	Water Resources Division
WRE	Water Resources Engineers, Inc.
μ	Micro (10^{-6})

CONTENTS

I. INTRODUCTION

During the past twenty years, the introduction of the electronic computer and the rapid hold that it has taken in practically every significant aspect of water resources technology has led to dramatic changes in the methodologies and practices of this field. Computer programs and systems have become an indispensable component of simulation and optimization models, of precipitation forecasting methods, of data collection activities, of functional procedures for the operation of river facilities, treatment plants, etc. Never before in the development of water recources technology has any device or concept exerted a comparable influence in so brief a time. The end is not in sight, as increasingly powerful facilities are created, and as the sophistication of programmers and users develops.

For this reason, it becomes urgent for the practitioners and decision-makers in the area of water resources—be they water resources planners, consultants, researchers, managers or legislators—to understand the role played by computers in water resources technology, and to assess the major issues connected with the introduction of computers for various purposes in a water resources system. The decision-makers also need to have an appreciation of the prospects for future development in computer technology, both software and hardware, and of their possible impact on water resources technology. Specifically, they must be able to answer such questions as:

- What are the roles of the computer—digital, analog, and hybrid—in research, development, planning, and operation of water resources systems? What specific characteristics of the computer make it suitable for a specific role? What developments are impossible without the computer? Are there situations of patent misuse due to a misunderstanding of computer characteristics and potential? How can the computer be used in an optimal fashion?
- What effect does the introduction of the computer have on the organizational structure of the groups using computers? What supporting activities are necessary for the effective use of computers? Are there significant patterns emerging from the current experiences that can guide future developments?

1

- What are the pros and cons of specific patterns of computer use? For example, when should a facility be time-shared? When should a library of computer programs be established? When should a computer be purchased new, or used, or leased? Are there specific needs of the water resources field in this connection?

The issues involved in answering questions of this kind are often extremely complex. Much of the necessary data are unavailable, and our knowledge concerning the management of computer and information systems is both embryonic and derived from contexts other than the water resources field. In effect, the computer has entered the technology of this field in a pragmatic and haphazard way: there has been a lack of overall planning and little attention paid—but for episodic cases—to gathering data and recording experiences that would provide a solid base for answering the needs of the practitioners and decision-makers.

This book does not pretend to cover the enormous breadth and depth of the computer's impact on the water resources field. Rather it is only an attempt—the first attempt, to the best of our knowledge—at assembling information and examining some of the principal issues that can provide a basis for answering the questions outlined above. Our task is simplified by the fact that regardless of which component of the water resources field one considers, many aspects governing the application of computers remain basically the same. For, in every area of water resources one deals in essence with the problems of physical description of the resource, of designing structures or processes that interact with the resource or control it (e.g., the introduction of pollutants or the damming of a river), of planning, management, and operation. In terms of a computer system, these problems resolve themselves in matters of data acquisition and management, analysis and design, and process control.

The considerations that emerge when one thinks *in terms of specific water resources areas* will be exemplified by surveying the use of the computer in three selected areas: surface water systems, groundwater systems, and water utilization systems. It will be evident from our survey that similar reviews of many other identifiable systems and subsystems, although desirable, would not add major new insights. As a consequence, the bulk of the book deals with the considerations that emerge when one looks at water resources systems *in terms of the computer*—considerations which cut across all areas of water resources technology. In essence, thus, this book can be viewed as a first exploration of the matrix in fig. 1-1, which considers the role of the computer both in terms of the water resource and of the basic tasks performed by the computer.

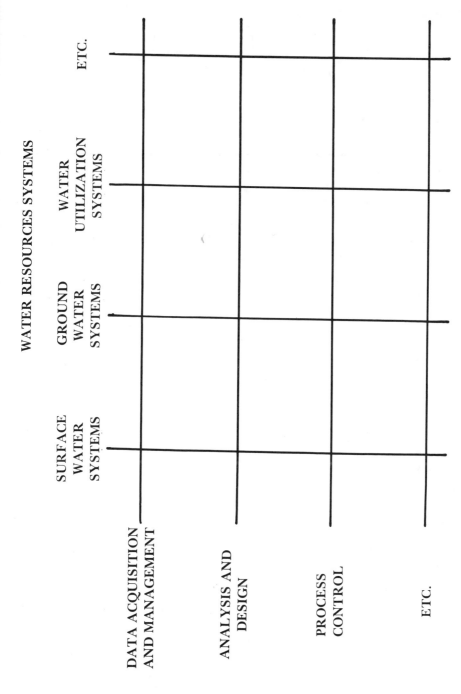

Fig. 1-1. The role of the computer in water resources; a matrix viewpoint.

THE GROWTH OF COMPUTERS

The explosive nature of the impact of computers on water resources technology can perhaps best be appreciated by reviewing the general trends in the production and utilization of digital computer systems—the systems that dominate the computer field.

In 1950 there were only 10 digital computers in existence in the United States. In 1973 there were over 100,000. The exact number is difficult to assess because statistics vary according to the source. For instance, the number of IBM computer installations as of July 1, 1969 was 20,244 or 29,388 or 35,491, depending on which census is accepted: *Computers and Automation* [1], *EDP Industry Report* [2], or *Automatic Data Processing Newsletter* [3].

The number of computers involved in water resources technology is also not easily assessed. The United States Corps of Engineers, the largest user of computers in this field, has approximately 40 dedicated computers. Considering the computers used in part for water resources work by the Bureau of Reclamation, universities, private consultants, etc., it may be assumed that over 1,000 computers are now involved totally or in part in water resources work in the United States. This growing utilization is indicated by the percentage of computer-oriented water resources work reported in selected engineering journals (table 1-1).

Table 1-1

Percentage of articles, in three selected publications,
reporting work in which computers played a major role

Publication	1960	1965	1970
Journal of the Hydraulics Division, ASCE	5%	14.5%	20.5%
Journal of the Sanitary Division, ASCE	0%	4.4%	21.4%
Water Resources Research	——	16.4%	26.9%

DIGITAL COMPUTERS AND MINICOMPUTERS

To assess the future role of the computer in water resources technology, it is useful to look at the world computer market, because trends in this market, rather than specific trends in the water resources field, are bound to exert a dominant influence on the type, size, and architecture of computer systems employed in the field.

It is estimated that in the U.S., about 30 billion dollars were invested in software and 20 billion in hardware as of 1969 [4]. Western Europe is the second largest user of computers (fig. 1-2), followed by Japan and the USSR [5]. By 1975, the total number of computers in these four major geographical areas is likely to reach a level between 200,000 and a quarter of a million (with a value near $96 billion [6]). The predominance of a single corporation—IBM—in this world market (table 1-2), has exerted a major influence on the development of hardware and software systems. However, recent action by the U.S. Supreme Court may alter this predominance.

The distribution of computers within the United States [7] (table 1-3), is also significant. The preponderance of manufacturing, service bureau,

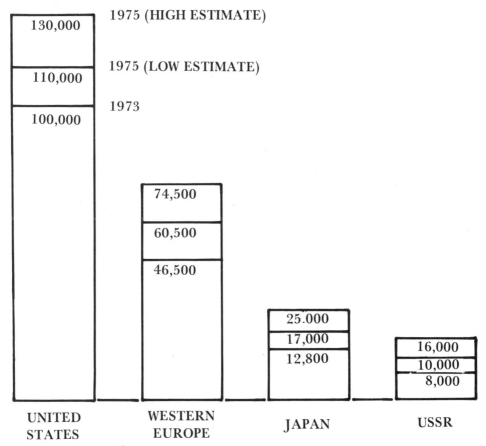

Fig. 1-2. Current and projected number of digital computer installations in major areas of the world (adapted from [5]).

Table 1-2

Percentage of world digital computer production by manufacturer (adapted from [5])

Medium and large computers	
IBM (International Business Machines)	57.0%
Honeywell-Bull	8.0%
Burroughs	5.5%
Univac	5.5%
NCR (National Cash Register)	5.1%
ICL (International Computers Limited)	2.3%
CDC (Control Data Corp)	2.0%
DEC (Digital Equipment Corp)	1.6%
Siemens	1.5%
XDS (Xerox Data Systems)	1.0%
Other	10.5%
Small and minicomputers	
DEC	41.0%
Honeywell-Bull	9.0%
Hewlett Packard	8.0%
Varian Data Systems	7.0%
General Automation	5.0%
Data General	4.0%
Other	26.0%

Table 1-3

Distribution of digital computers within the United States (adapted from [7])

Area	% Total installed 1/1/73	% Growth 1972
Manufacturing	29.2	-1
Service Bureaus	12.5	6
Federal Govt.	11.8	11
Banking & Financial	11.6	4
Insurance	6.5	-2
Education	6.4	1
State & Local Govt.	5.2	17
Communications & Utilities	5.0	3
Wholesale	5.0	3
Transportation Carriers	3.1	7
Retail	2.6	5
Medical & Health Services	1.6	10
Other	0.8	14

Source: International Data Corp.

banking, and governmental usage indicates that the needs of these fields are likely to dominate future developments, particularly of large computer systems. Essentially the same distribution characterizes Western Europe and Japan.

An area of increasing importance both in water resources and in the general world market is that of small computers and minicomputers. Since these computers have made and will make an impact quite distinct from that of the larger installations, in this book they will generally be discussed separately. Growth predictions by major area of utilization are shown in fig. 1-3 [8] ; the projected increase in the area of data handling is particularly noteworthy. (It must be remembered, however, that the aggregate computing power and workload of the smaller computers remains much less than that of the larger computers.)

At present there are in the world over 60 manufacturers of minicomputers; the major ones are shown in table 1-2 and listed in Appendix 1 [9]. The field is dominated by the Digital Equipment Corporation which accounts for approximately 40% of the total number of computers. The activity of IBM in this area, conversely, is quite limited, although it may not remain so.

ANALOG AND HYBRID COMPUTERS

Trends in analog and hybrid production are much more dependent on the general economic trends in specific areas, such as educational and government spending. Up to the mid 50's most analog computers were special-purpose machines, but general-purpose machines began to emerge rapidly thereafter.

In general, the cost of an analog computer depends primarily on the number of amplifiers it contains, and to a lesser extent on the desired accuracy, which may be of the order of 0.01% in the larger systems. The costs range from $4000-6000 for a computer with 5 to 10 amplifiers, suitable for the solution of simple problems, to $200,000-500,000 for systems with several hundred amplifiers, suitable for simulation and solution of complex systems of differential equations [10]. The complexity of most water resources problems that can be solved on an analog computer generally favors incorporation of the analog into a hybrid system, in which the analog is linked to a digital computer. In this configuration, the total cost (including the digital computer) can be $600,000-900,000 or higher, depending on the cost of the digital computer. It is interesting to note that hybridization has even been extended to the smaller systems by providing them with limited digital logic functions, as exemplifed by the MiniAC computer [11].

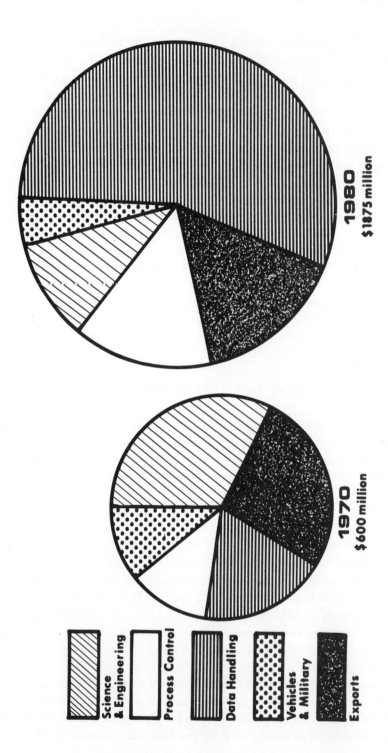

Fig. 1-3. Small and minicomputer growth predictions including major areas of utilization [8]. Reprinted with permission of Datamation ® Copyright 1971 by Technical Publishing Company, Greenwich, Connecticut 06830.

Two major analog and hybrid computer manufacturers are Electronic Associates, Inc. (EAI) and Applied Dynamics Computer Systems, with the former maintaining a 50% to 70% predominance of the world market [11]. The average production of EAI over the last decade was $40 million/year in the United States and $20 million/year elsewhere. The projection for world production by the same company for the period 1975-80 is $80 million/ year, maintaining approximately the same ratio between U.S. and non-U.S. distribution. The approximate total number of systems produced by EAI for the period 1962-72 is given in fig. 1-4. The European analog and hybrid computer market has been estimated at $29.5 million for 1972 and $32.1 million for 1973 [12], representing approximately a 10% growth for the year.

The major users of analog and hybrid systems are in the fields of education, industry, government, and government-related activities. The net

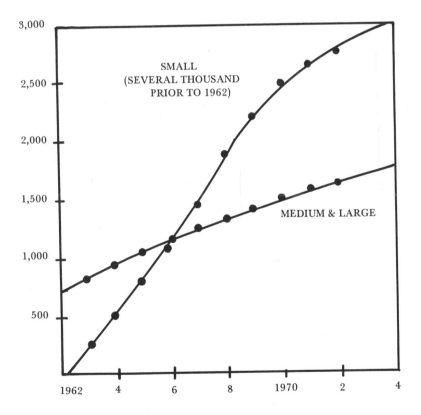

Fig. 1-4.   The approximate number of analog and hybrid computers manufactuered by Electronics Associates, Inc. (based on [11]).

worth (number of computers times computer price) of analog computers in
each of these four major fields is approximately equal, although exact
numbers are not currently available. The larger systems are primarily utilized
in government and government-related areas, while most of the small analogs
are used in the educational field. The pattern has a significant impact on the
utilization of analog and hybrid computers in water resources, since
engineering students, who are prospective water resources workers, have an
opportunity to become familiar only with the smaller, less sophisticated
analogs, while having access to very large and sophisticated digital
computers. Thus, they carry into their professional activities the feeling that
the analog is a small, unsophisticated tool.

COMPUTER USERS

In assessing the role of computer technology in the water resources field,
it is desirable to consider the organizations actively involved. The
organizations in the field that use computer systems can be categorized as
falling into three groups:

Governmental—Multi-National, Federal, State, and Local
Private—Consulting Firms, Utilities, and Industries
Independent—Universities and Research Centers

The areas of involvement of selected organizations in these categories are
indicated in table 1-4. The table maintains the structure of the matrix
presented earlier and summarizes the organizational details that follow. On a
coarse quantitative scale, "X" denotes involvement and "XX" extensive
involvement.

GOVERNMENTAL ORGANIZATIONS

In general, throughout the world, governmental organizations have
responsibility for the major portion of expenditures on water resources
activities, as well as for the planning, construction, and control of most
physical facilities (reservoirs, dams, treatment plants, etc.). Central
organizations are extensively involved in planning and research and perform
most of the data acquisition functions. Local organizations are particularly
involved in planning, construction, and control of water supply and water
treatment facilities.

In describing the nature of some of these organizations, we shall dwell
more on organizations actively performing computational functions, such as
the Environmental Protection Agency (EPA), rather than those, such as the
Office of Water Resources Research (OWRR), which coordinate and control

Table 1-4

Major area of involvement by organization

Organization	Surface Water			Groundwater			Utilization		
	DA&M	A&D	PC	DA&M	A&D	PC	DA&M	A&D	PC
BR	X	XX	XX	X	X	X		X	X
CE	X	XX	XX	X	X	X	X	XX	XX
CE-HEC		XX			X			XX	
EPA-ERL	X	XX		X	X	XX			
EPA-WPO	XX	X		XX			X		
GS-WRD	XX	X		XX			XX	X	
HYDC		XX			X			XX	
HYDS		XX			X			XX	
NOAA	X						X		
NWS	X						X		
QLM		XX			X		X	XX	
SCS				X	XX	X			
TVA	X	X	XX				X	X	XX
UNIV	X	XX		X	XX		X	XX	
WRE		XX		X	XX			XX	

DA&M; Data Acquisition and Management: A&D; Analysis and Design: PC; Process Control

research activities (this, of course, in no way implies that one kind of organization is more important than the other). Emphasis has also been placed on the engineering and operational aspects, rather than on administrative functions. A list of the computer facilities located in major U.S. governmental organizations is given in Appendix 2.

An example of the broad range of activities in which a governmental agency can be involved is offered by the Bureau of Reclamation (BR) in the United States. The Bureau's engineering and research center in Denver specializes in planning, design, construction, operation, and maintenance of water resources facilities for arid and semi-arid land in 17 western states. Some of the more recent projects which involve extensive reliance on computers include: determination, using aerial photographs and other parameters, of the amount of acreage suitable for irrigation; utilization of linear programming to determine farm budgets; computer analysis of concrete dams to include aesthetic aspects; atmospheric water research or "rain-making" [13]. The Bureau currently (1973) uses an in-house Honeywell 800/200 computer. However, a recent survey indicated that about one-third of the automatic data processing (ADP) budget went to outside service contracts; as a result, the Bureau is in the process of acquiring a new system [14]. Most field offices of the Bureau are connected to the Computer Sciences Corporation (CSC INFONET) utility, which is used for engineering applications. The Denver center supports the computer activities of the offices and extensive laboratory facilities [15], as well as the Bureau of Reclamation Engineering Computer System (BRECS) program library (see Chapter III and Appendix 7).

Another example of a government organization heavily involved in computer usage—primarily for data collection and analysis—is the U.S. Geological Survey (USGS). The major objectives of its Water Resources Division (WRD) are to provide data collection facilities (see Data Acquisition and Management, Chapter IV), as well as to appraise the quantity, quality, and availability of water resources so that rational decisions about water development, flood protection, pollution control, etc., can be made. Representative research projects include [16]:

- Methodologies for accurately predicting temperature variation that results from thermal loading in lakes and streams
- Computer simulations of: one dimensional transient flows in waterways; movement of wavecrests in open channels; unsteady, free-surface, gravity flow through porous media induced by transient open-channel flow
- Studies involving the application of unsaturated flow theory to drainage and infiltration
- Development of deterministic models for transient flow through porous media
- Stochastic modeling for storm events to determine the reliability of flood-frequency relationships in small watersheds and time and space-dependent seasonal flows.

To accomplish these and other projects, the USGS acquired an IBM 370/155 to be used primarily for scientific work at Reston, Virginia. The computer is linked to an IBM 360/65B in Washington, which gives USGS great potential for service to the 70 or so terminals connected to the system (see Appendix 3 for details). These terminals, mostly of the remote job entry (RJE) type, range from low speed teletype terminals to high speed IBM 1130's and 360/20's, that represent substantial computational power. Twenty-four of the terminals exclusively serve water resources users. The overall annual cost for these computer facilities at WRD is about $1.5 million or approximately 2% of the $73 million 1973 budget.

PRIVATE ORGANIZATIONS

A substantial portion of the analysis and design of water resources systems is performed by private firms. A typical firm might have 10-40 professionals with a substantial portion of these holding advanced degrees, particularly in the companies dealing with the less routine problems. Typically, these firms perform analyses for projects in the $10,000 to $1 million range. Since most are smaller organizations, they often find it uneconomical to support an in-house computer facility; hence many have RJE or interactive terminals connected to a computer utility or locally-available computer. A substantial amount of the work is computer-oriented, making "turn-around-time" an important consideration. It is difficult to estimate the number of firms that are involved in at least some aspects of computer usage in water resources. A small list of some typical U.S. firms that have become involved in computer modeling and analysis is given in Appendix 4.

An example of a firm which specializes in computer applications for water resources planning and design is Hydrocomp. This company, with a professional staff of approximately 15 (in 1973), half of which are Ph.D.'s or M.S.'s, is organized to assist consulting firms and other engineering organizations in system simulations [17]. Some specific areas of the firm's interest include simulation of streamflow records and water quality, hydrologic network design, groundwater replenishment studies, reservoir planning and operation, water supply forecasting, urban stormwater flows, and flood plain mapping. Unlike other private firms, a substantial portion of their business is derived from leasing software. The Hydrocomp Simulation Program (HSP), adapted from a watershed model developed at Stanford by one of the principals of the firm (see Digital Watershed Simulation, Chapter V), is available on several major computer utilities. A support center is maintained to answer inquiries about program operations, output, and error messages, as well as to provide on-line consulting services. Workshops are held to provide users with a basic understanding of the programs.

Another example of a company with extensive computer involvement (estimated at 90% of all projects) is Water Resources Engineers. The firm has a professional staff of 35, also with a high proportion of graduate degree holders [18]. One outcome of their activities has been a sizeable program library on such subjects as hydraulic behavior of estuaries, stratified reservoirs, pipe networks, flood routing, resource allocation, reservoir operation, conservative pollutants in groundwater, cost-benefit analysis, and impact of water shortages. Most work is done via an RJE terminal to a computer utility (Information System Design, ISD) which operates a Univac 1108.

A third example is provided by Hydroscience, a subsidiary of Dow Chemical Company with a staff of 40 professionals (in 1973), which specializes in pollution control problems [19] and utilizes an in-house IBM

1130 with a core capacity of 16,000 words. The effort of the company·has been directed toward the areas of natural water systems analysis, process design, research and development, environmental management studies, and analytical investigations. The computer effort, estimated at 50-60% of all activities, centers on waste treatment design and process development, water analysis, systems and management design, environmental impact studies, and related pollution control problems. An extensive program library has resulted from these activities.

All of these examples are clearly what can be considered high-technology companies. Although in a sense they are not typical, they are relevant to our study because they portray different roles and modes of computer utilization—from a computer-service-oriented company to a company relying heavily on RJE terminal service to a company utilizing an in-house computer.

INDEPENDENT ORGANIZATIONS

The category of independent organizations includes the many academic and research institutions actively involved in solving water resources problems. Typically these institutions use their own computer facilities and are characterized by advanced hardware as well as considerable software innovation (text editors, graphics, etc.). The water resources involvement is generally more in the research area than in the operational area and has led to advances in methodologies and applications.

OVERVIEW

It is evident that the future use of computers in water resources technology will be influenced by trends in computer production and in the activities of the major computer users. Some of the significant factors include:

- The overwhelming predominance of digital over analog and hybrid computers (total world market estimates are 98% digital, 1% analog, 1% hybrid [7]).
- The explosive growth in the production of inexpensive mini-computers.
- The predominance, among the producers of larger digital computer systems, of one corporation. A similar situation exists in the areas of minicomputers and of analog computers, but the smaller capital investments required in these areas may make future trends more volatile.

- The fact that the educational experiences of persons preparing for careers in water resources tend to develop greater familiarity with sophisticated digital rather than sophisticated analog computers. This exerts a subtle but significant influence on the selection and use of computers in water resources.
- In the field operations of a water resources organization, the advantages of utilizing a large centralized computer facility seem to outweigh the advantages of diverse non-connected computer installations.
- At the same time, the versatility offered by minicomputers, both isolated and in an interconnected system.
- The strong position that computer utilities will maintain in the future, as evidenced by the growing number of smaller organizations that are employing remote job entry terminals.
- The availability from utilities of package programs which offer a viable alternative to ad hoc programming, provided adequate training is given in how to correctly utilize the larger programs.

REFERENCES

[1] Monthly Computer Census, *Computers and Automation,* 19, 1970, 68-69.
[2] Monthly Computer Census, *EDP Industry Report,* September 11, 1969, 11.
[3] Diebold Semi-Annual Computer Census, *Automatic Data Processing Newsletter,* September 22, 1969, 3-4.
[4] Bemer, R.W., Manageable Software, In: J.T. Tou (Editor), *Software Engineering,* Academic Press, New York, 1970, p. 124.
[5] Statistiques 1972, *L'EXPANSION,* 54, 1972, 62-65.
[6] United Nations Department of Economics and Social Affairs, *The Application of Computer Technology for Development,* Publ. No. E. 71. II. A.1, 1971, p. 77.
[7] Standard and Poor's, Office Equipment Systems and Services, Industry Surveys, June 14, 1973, 11-21.
[8] Gross, C., Accessibility and the Small Computer, *Datamation,* 17, 1971, 42-48.
[9] Hillegas, J.R., The minicomputer—getting it all together, *Computer Decisions,* 4, 1972, 36-39.
[10] Datamation Magazine, Datamation 1972 EDP Industry Directory, 1972.
[11] Kaplan, W., personal communications, Manager of Business Planning and Development, Electronic Associates, Inc., West Long Branch, New Jersey, 1973.
[12] European 1973 Equipment Markets, *ELECTRONICS,* 45, 1972, 85.
[13] Burton, L., internal communications, received from C. Furgeson, Bureau of Reclamation, Denver, Colorado, 1973.
[14] Furgeson, C., personal communications, Bureau of Reclamation, Denver, Colorado, 1973.
[15] Engle, P., personal communications, Bureau of Reclamation, Denver, Colorado, 1973.
[16] U.S. Geological Survey, internal communications, received from S. Lang, U.S. Geological Survey, Reston, Va., 1973.
[17] Crawford, N.H., personal communications, President, Hydrocomp, Inc., Palo Alto, California, 1973.
[18] Evenson, D., personal communications, Manager, Water Resources Engineers, Inc., Walnut Creek, California, 1973.
[19] Thomann, R.V., personal communications, Associate, Hydroscience, Inc., Westwood, New Jersey, 1973.

II. THE ELEMENTS OF A COMPUTER SYSTEM

This chapter discusses the elements of computer systems as well as some of the basic concepts governing their employ, with a constant view towards water resources applications.

COMPUTER HARDWARE

DIGITAL COMPUTERS

The digital computer is most effectively used when massive data handling and computations are required. It is generally composed of three major elements—the processor (CPU, or central processing unit), the memory, and the input/output (I/O) devices (fig. 2-1).

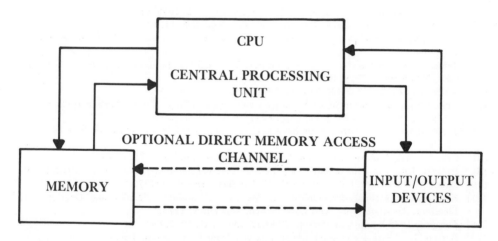

Fig. 2-1. The three basic elements of a digital computer.

The immediate forerunner of the electronic computer was an electro-mechanical computer, the Harvard Mark I, that became operational in 1944. Soon thereafter, electron tubes were employed, followed in the early 50's by transistors, which dominated computer design until the mid 60's when integrated circuits became the most salient feature of computer hardware. This evolution of computer technology has led to order of magnitude increases in the performance of the computer; a quantity measured, for instance, by the ratio of the capacity of computer memory to the time required for addition (fig. 2-2). The increased performance has been due primarily to the concurrence of three factors:

- A dramatic improvement in the number of logical elements per unit volume in the central processor. Ten years ago, one "and/or" gate per silicon chip was the norm; 5 years ago, the density had increased to 100 gates per chip; today, experimental design can achieve from 600 to 3,000 gates per silicon chip. By 1980, densities of 10,000 gates per chip are foreseeable. This will enormously reduce the size of the central processor.
- The decreased cost of logical elements. The cost of $2.00 per gate before 1960 has become about $0.03 per gate in 1973. By the late 70's, costs of less than $0.01 per gate can be expected. As a result, the current cost constraints have been switched from the gate technology to the packaging technology—i.e., how to package extremely large numbers of gates in small volumes.
- The increase in capacity and speed of memories. In the mid 50's memory capacity was typically between 100,000 and 1,000,000 bits and memory speed was 10 microseconds (μsec.). In the mid 60's, the capacity of the largest units varied between 1,000,000 and 10,000,000 bits, with speeds of about 1 μsec. The systems of the mid 70's have capacities higher than a trillion bits with speeds of 10^{-2} μsec. On the other hand, the memory elements most widely used today are still ferro-magnetic, some with moving parts, which provide a constraining factor. In the near future, other techniques, such as the magnetic bubble technique, are expected to provide the possibility of storing a million digits per square centimeter of garnet crystal.

Another significant element of the improved performance of the computer is the mean time between failures (MTBF), which in early computers was of the order of 20 seconds to 30 minutes and is now of the order of months in large centralized systems, and of years in minicomputers.

The combination of a miniaturized and inexpensive central processor and highly dense, low cost memories makes it likely that by 1978 very powerful computers will come into operation at costs of less than $10,000.

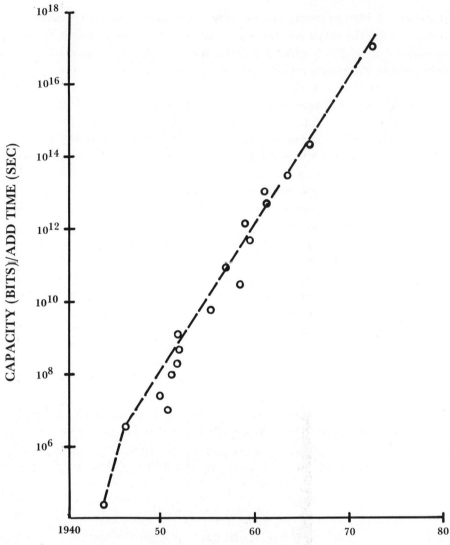

Fig. 2-2.   General trends in computer evolution.

Processor

The processor performs the control and computational functions, is generally characterized by its size, computation time, and special capabilities, and has a price ranging over 3 orders of magnitude (fig. 2-3 [1]). Most larger machines have multiple processors to provide for more effective distribution of the work load. The CDC 6600, for example, has up to ten peripheral processors which control various I/O devices, and a single control processor which performs sequential processing of programmed instructions. On the other hand, the Memorex/40, a recent development, has eight processors [2], three of which function independently and are available to run simultaneous programs.

These multiple processor devices must be distinguished from parallel processors, in which multiple processors simultaneously perform parts of the *same program*. The Illiac IV is currently the ultimate realization of this concept, incorporating sixty-four synchronous processors, and is best suited to matrix or array operations. The complete add time for 64 simultaneous additions (e.g., two 8 x 8 matrices) is .625 μsec. (comparable to a *single* addition in other systems) or .0098 μsec. per addition [3].

Despite individual variations, all the systems mentioned so far operate in a step-wise single instruction mode. The pipeline processor, realized in the CDC STAR (STring-ARray) computer, is a new system operating on a totally different conceptual basis. It consists of four multiple-stage pipe or assembly lines, with an incoming data rate of up to 100 million 32 bit operands per second [3]. The system performs functional operations on vectors containing both data and instructions. Though the control of the pipelines is undoubtedly more complex than that required of other processors, the extremely high throughput speed of the system suggests that it will have revolutionary abilities.

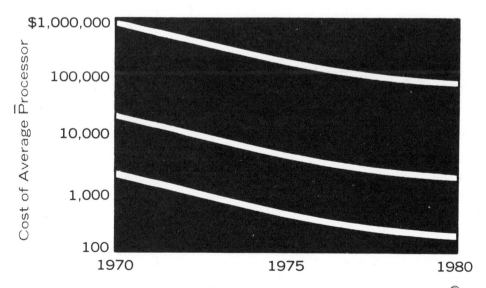

Fig. 2-3. The trends in the cost of processors [1]. Reprinted with permission of Datamation ®
Copyright 1973 by Technical Publishing Company, Greenwich, Connecticut 06830.

Memory

The second major element of the digital computer, the memory, is the storage facility for all data and instructions, and is characterized by speed (access or cycle time), capacity (total number of bits or words of storage), and method of address (direct, indirect, associative, etc.). Of the three most common types of memory—core, disc, and magnetic tape—core storage provides the fastest cycle time, typically from 10 to .75 μsec. Core storage is generally formatted in terms of words, which are made up of bits, and is expandable from 4k (4096 words x number of bits per word = total bit storage) to 512k in the larger systems. At the sacrifice of some speed, increased capacity can be attained by replacing the high speed core with an Extended Core Memory (ECM) or a Large Capacity Storage (LCS) device. A resulting 1024k memory, for example, might have a typical access time ranging from 8 to 2.8 μsec. [4] .

Disc storage, on the other hand, provides large capacity, typically ranging from 7 to 28 megabytes (1 byte = 8 bits) per disc pack. The loss of access speed in disc storage is generally compensated for by its lower cost per bit, typically $0.001/bit compared to $0.10/bit for core (based on an average of four commercially available disc and core systems). Disc and core storage may be combined in a "virtual" memory [5] , where part of a large program is stored on disc and interchanged or "swapped" with the contents of core whenever required. This process "effectively" increases the core size and, as a result of IBM's incorporating this principle in its new systems, has generated much interest.

Magnetic tape is generally used as a "library" or rarely accessed storage device, because it must be read sequentially. A complete routine stored on tape can be loaded into the system and then executed without reaccessing the tape. Often, magnetic tape is used as a buffer between the high speed central processor and low speed devices such as card readers and line printers, a process commonly known as "off-lining" these devices. Card images, for example, are read onto tape and later transferred to the processor at a much faster rate. This buffering concept can readily be extended to water resources data collection. Data taken from low speed devices and sensors at remote sites can be recorded on tape in "real time" and then transferred, either by mail or telephone line, to the processing center. Such an approach is becoming increasingly attractive because of the recent commercial development of moderately priced cassette tape recording systems that offer a very economical alternative (priced at less than $1,000) to large multi-track recorders that cost around $5,000.

There are several new devices which suggest possible future trends in storage equipment. The cache or scratch pad memory, originally introduced in the IBM 360/85, is a limited capacity, very high speed memory for recently accessed storage words. The conceptual basis of the cache is that recently accessed (requested) words are likely to be reaccessed. Statistical evidence does, in fact, show that if a few thousand words are stored in the cache, well over 90% of future accesses will be from the cache rather than the main memory [6]. Other trends in optical mass memories [7], solid state and thin planar memories [8], magnetic buble memories, and hybrid associative memories [9] indicate the coming availability of very large yet very fast memory systems. Fig. 2-4 graphically depicts these technological trends away from the predominant core memory [8].

Input/Output (I/O)

The third element of a digital computer system is the Input/Output (I/O) equipment, composed mainly of card readers, line printers, CRT displays, etc. These devices, which are generally described in terms of their most important feature, speed (cards per minute, lines per minute, etc.), are not of great consequence unless extremely large amounts of input and output are required. Looking to the future, of greater consequence to the technology of I/O devices are developments in graphic display techniques that emphasize ease of understanding and interaction with the computer.

MINICOMPUTERS (MINIS)

Minicomputers, a recent development, are exerting a major influence on the computer industry and on the use of computers. They possess distinctive characteristics which make it desirable to discuss them apart from the larger computer systems.

A typical minicomputer is a parallel, binary processor with a 16 bit word length. It generally offers from 4k to 32k words of storage housed in a compact cabinet weighing less than 50 pounds. Its price tag may be about $5,000 with substantial discounts for quantity purchases. It is often characterized by faster computation times, cassette tape memory systems, small disc memory systems, and simple low speed card readers and line printers. Though disc storage may be desired, the cost of a disc system and required controller may easily exceed the cost of the mini and can lead to a storage-heavy, inflexible system. The emergence of economical floppy disc systems may resolve this problem.

A consideration that can be critical when establishing a minicomputer

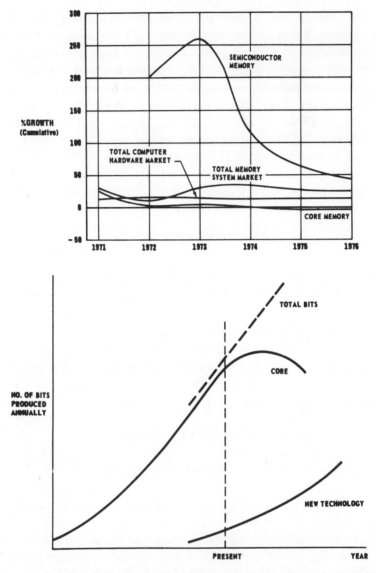

Fig. 2-4. Trends in memory growth by percentage growth (top) and qualitatively (bottom) [8].
Reprinted with permission of Datamation ® Copyright 1971 by Technical Publishing
Company, Greenwich, Connecticut 06830.

installation is that of peripheral devices. Most minicomputer manufacturers
do not make such devices, and those commercially available are often not
compatible. It may be necessary for a user either to purchase a commercially
available interface to make the particular peripheral device compatible with

the mini, or to have an interface manufactured ad hoc. Other important questions concern maintenance and software support.

Although a large number of minicomputers cost less than $10,000, the range extends upwards to $100,000. Within these limits, a great variety of designs and capabilities are encountered. In addition to the list of minicomputer manufacturers given in Appendix 1, a list of peripheral device manufacturers is given by Murphy [10]. All minis incorporate, or are capable of incorporating, processors, memories, and I/O devices. However, they perform most efficiently when the memory and I/O functions are minimized. Since extensive I/O software is generally required to drive even the simplest device, a great deal of memory and process time would be dedicated to I/O functions, thus reducing the general efficacy of the minicomputer. This is especially true of the very "stripped" minis.

Currently the largest market for minicomputers is in industrial control, data communications, research, and education; specifically including automatic testing and inspection, numerical control of machine tools, peripheral controllers for larger computers, programmable communication terminals, and multistation keyboard entry devices for entry to larger computer systems. The area of conventional business data processing remains, however, an elusive market [11]. The impact of minis in such areas as process control [10-13] or centralized systems is substantial and will be discussed later.

One of the most significant effects of the introduction of minicomputers is the breaking-loose of the organizational structure under which computers have been operating. The centralized computer center was the product of computer systems of high cost, which, to amortize the high fixed charges, had to be run around the clock. The minicomputer, with its low fixed charges, remains economical with low utilization factors and is intrinsically more efficient than a large computer, in which up to 80% of the core storage is required to mastermind the organization of a task. These factors will make computer centers necessary only for the collection, management, and distribution of data and programs, and for computational tasks of great complexity. Fig. 2-5 [14] shows how, with increases in complexity of a computational task, the cost of minicomputer solutions increases, while that of "maxicomputer" solutions decreases, indicating that the maxicomputer is irreplaceable for the solution of complex problems.

ANALOG COMPUTERS

The analog computer is most effectively used in solving problems stated

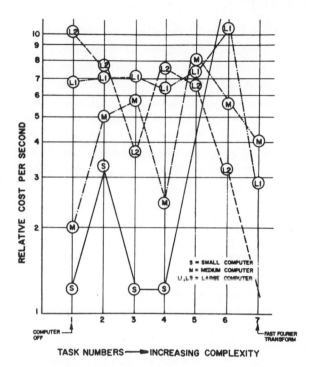

Fig. 2-5. Computational costs as a function of task complexity for computers of different size [14]. Reprinted from Electronics, March 29, 1971; Copyright McGraw-Hill, Inc., 1971.

in terms of integral/differential equations, and in simulating complex physical systems [15]. It is composed of amplifiers—which serve as integrators, summers (adders), and multipliers—and are patched or wired together to represent a problem. Where the digital computer generally performs operations sequentially and can store a complete record of any operation, the analog performs simultaneous operations and has essentially no memory facilities (though many of the larger analog computers have several digital registers and counters). Since a digital computer is basically an adder, it must use a numerical approximation method to solve differential equations, where the analog, itself composed of integrators, can produce a continuous exact solution. As the complexity of a problem increases, the *time* required for a digital (sequential) solution increases; whereas the corresponding analog (simultaneous) solution requires only an increased *number* of amplifiers acting in parallel, with no increase in the time required.

The analog computer, simulating a physical system, can produce solutions in real time. The flexibility of its time scale, however, allows real time to be slowed down or speeded up—i.e., converting seconds to hours or years to minutes. A time-dependent voltage (sine wave, square wave, etc.)

generally serves as the analog input (forcing function), and can be supplied by generators within the computer or external sources (motor tachometers, etc.). The analog output is a time-varying output whose magnitude (with appropriate scale factors) represents a function, its derivatives, or some combination of these. This continuous output can be observed on a plotter or CRT, or used as a control signal for other devices.

HYBRID COMPUTERS

There are few scientific problems that are either purely analog or purely digital; force-fitting analog problems onto a digital computer, or vice-versa, has led to disastrous results. To avoid this pitfall, hybrid computer systems, composed of both a digital and an analog computer, linked by a mating interface and incorporating the best features of both, have been developed. The accuracy, memory, and capacity of the digital is combined with the speed of the analog. Where, in the purely digital system, the operator *needs no* knowledge of the program, but is only required to initiate it, the analog operator generally *does* require some knowledge of the program for execution. The operator of a hybrid system, on the other hand, is often the engineer, and can effectively interact with the program, probing, refining, and changing the variables, thus becoming part of the loop in a three-way dialogue: man—computer—program.

The need to use nonlinear partial differential equations with irregular boundary conditions to describe or simulate certain aspects of hydrologic systems (for example water flow in the saturated and nonsaturated zones of geological formations, streamflow routing, or reservoir routing) provides the purely analog or purely digital-oriented engineer with a dilemma. Digital solutions require unusually long and complicated computer runs to reach desired accuracy; the analog approach is generally complicated by the presence in the equation of more than one independent variable [16]. Unlike either of its component computers, the hybrid computer is readily adaptable to this type of problem.

The digital component of a hybrid system generally must have high-speed input/output data and interrupt terminals connected through a controller (linkage) to the analog computer. The controller translates digital instructions into corresponding physical and electrical connections in the analog computer, as well as coordinating data transfers [17]. A "true hybrid" [15] is characterized by intimate hardware connections between computers, and generally requires a sophisticated controller. In a true hybrid, ideally, both computers can issue commands and transfer data bilaterally. Thus the digital can "address" various components of the analog computer (integrators, summers, potentiometers, etc.) and either "read" them or set them to a specific value. There are, however, a great number of hybrid systems—"conceptual hybrids"—with a more limited scope of operation that allow digital sampling but generally lack control commands.

Input/output operations take on new dimensions in a true hybrid system. Continuous analog outputs can be plotted as well as sampled and printed. The continuous output of the analog can be sampled by the digital, operated upon numerically, and then fed back to the analog as a forcing function. Though certain delays are unavoidable and must be taken into account [15], the value of this last characteristic cannot be overstressed for the solution of certain simulation problems in water resources. A powerful controller, an analog computer with hundreds of amplifiers, and a set of carefully selected analog to digital (A-D) and digital to analog (D-A) converters [18] combined with a medium sized digital computer, can provide the user with a sophisticated tool for solving problems by variation of parameters, iterative techniques, etc.

MODELS

In the area of analogs and hybrids and, to a lesser extent, digitals, a distinction should be made between computers (on which a problem may be modelled) and ad hoc models. Generally an analog (or hybrid) *computer* is programmed (or wired) to model a system, and makes it possible to analyze the results of varying the parameters of the system. Analyzing a different system is accomplished simply by reprogramming (rewiring) the computer. Often this is done by removing the programming panel on the analog and replacing it with a panel wired for the new problem.

On the other hand, an ad hoc analog or hybrid *model* generally lacks this flexibility. It is a dedicated model of the system, often consisting of discrete electronic components (resistors, capacitors, transistors, etc.) connected in an elaborate network; for example, the Biscayne Aquifer, Houston, and Anchorage models of the U.S. Geological Survey [19]. An important historical example of such a model is the McIlroy Analyzer, used for piping networks [20]. Generally, an ad hoc model is useful only in simulating a particular system and would require major changes for adaption to a new problem. The model can verge on being a computer, or vice versa, especially when an elaborate model and dedicated computer are intimately connected, as exemplified by the Kitakami River flood simulator [21].

HARDWARE CONSIDERATIONS

The Man-Machine Interface

As the size, speed, and complexity of computer systems increase, the problem of an effective user-machine interface acquires increasing importance. It does not suffice to consider the problem as one of producing faster card readers and line printers to keep up with the computer, although these have their place; rather it is a problem of making the modes of input and output more interactive. Prime examples are the developments of the last decade in the area of visual display. The cathode ray tube (CRT) and similar graphics terminals have greatly increased the flexibility and efficiency with which the user can approach the computer. A specific example is the INSIGHT (Interactive System for Investigation by Graphics of Hydrological Trends) Program developed by Phillips [22] at the University of Michigan for graphically interpreting STORET data. The advent of multicolor displays can play a useful role in depicting trends that result from environmental impact studies. These displays are especially useful when attempting to explain the consequences of certain actions to the layman. In water resources, the use of these displays has been very limited, and systematic research on the development of the most effective man-computer interfaces to suit the needs of the field has been practically non-existent. Yet, it would be highly desirable to improve optical scanning of terrain maps for purposes such as construction planning or flood plain management. It would also be desirable to computerize visual modes of representation and monitoring, e.g., for the purpose of improving river traffic management or the operation of a piping network.

Computer-Instrument Packages

A major issue in the area of hardware arises from the development of intimately connected computer-instrument packages, made possible by the new and inexpensive "stripped minis" and microcomputer sets [23]. A *stripped mini* is a complete minicomputer with a 1k to 4k (by 8 bit) memory, a limited instruction repertoire, and costing about $2,000-4,000. A *microcomputer set* is an extremely inexpensive dedicated unit assembled from several components—a central processing unit (CPU) and appropriate instruction memory and data memory chips—which can be programmed for a specific utilization. Typical microcomputer component costs [24] are (depending on quantity):

4 bit CPU with 45 Instructions	$30- 60
8 bit CPU with 49 Instructions	$60-180
256 instruction Read-Only Memory (ROM)	$15- 25
256 instruction Programmable ROM (PROM)	$65-100
320 bit data Random Access Memory (RAM)	$15- 30

The component approach reduces the cost of a computer (including power supplies, printed circuit boards, etc.) to less than $1,000 [25] and may be as significant to instrumentation packages as it currently is to the calculator industry.

A *computer-instrument package* is a system in which a computer is intimately connected with an instrument package sensitive to environmental or other variables. This connection can occur at several levels of sophistication; three of these are (fig. 2-6):

1) sensor + microcomputer components (the "under $1,000" level)
2) sensor + complete "stripped mini" (the "$2,000" level)
3) sensor + complete minicomputer, usually at some distance from the sensor (the "$5,000" level)

At the first level of sophistication, the incorporation of economical logic and memory elements into sensor-controller devices enables these devices to perform limited logical tasks on data (preprocessing, compressing, formatting), as well as to control and monitor gates, pumps, dosimeters, etc. Water quality measurements requiring a complex series of tests to generate an "index" of the measured quantity are ideally suited to this type of package. Trends at this level are increasing programmability and improved input/output features, which are becoming available on commercial instrumentation.

With the introduction of instrument packages with a complete stripped mini—at the second level of sophistication—the operation of a myriad of field devices and instrument stations can be automated. The stripped mini, replacing discrete elements as the basic building block, provides the user with increased power and software flexibility. Decisions based on the analysis of current operating conditions can be implemented "on the spot", reducing the reliance on centralized control systems and the inherent possibility of communciation or system failures.

At the third level of sophistication, connection of the instrumentation to a minicomputer offers almost unlimited power at the data collection site. When the site is the laboratory, the sensor is a laboratory instrument (e.g., a spectrometer); a minicomputer, often combined with a visual display and cassette recorder, can usually analyze the data in milliseconds, and thus allows the experimenter to alter the procedure while the experiment is in progress. It also eliminates human error and provides an accurate record of

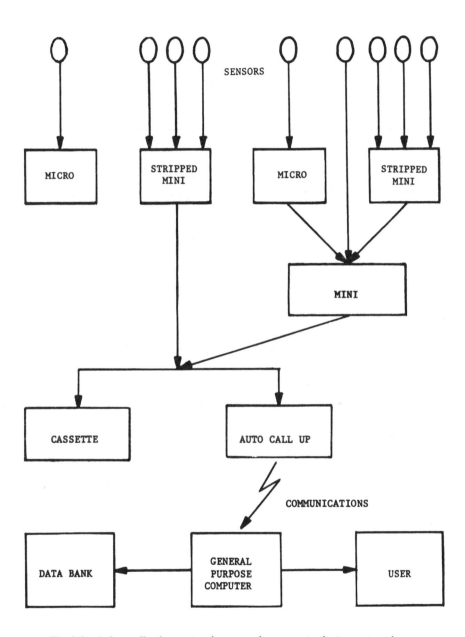

Fig. 2-6. A data collection system incorporating computer-instrument packages.

the data. The versatility and peripheral equipment required for this type of operation often increases the price of the computer system to the $10,000-15,000 range. As an example of laboratory use of computer-instrument packages, the Southeast Environmental Research Laboratory of the EPA has a mass spectrometer, gas chromatograph and minicomputer linked together, which makes it possible to identify organic compounds in a water sample within a few hours [26]. The Bureau of Reclamation has been using a General Automation SPC-12 connected to laboratory sensors, and because of the favorable experience with this arrangement, it has now acquired a multi-minicomputer system to tie together its five laboratories [27]. Another example is the recent (Dec., 73) connection of a laser spectrometer and other instrumentation to a DEC GT40 at the U.S. Geological Survey, which allows on-the-spot data analysis, and thus immediate refinement of tests and procedures [28]. An installation at the Iowa Institute of Hydraulic Research, utilizing an IBM 1801, employs the same concepts but represents a system much larger than those considered in the previous examples [29].

Maintenance

In the decisions concerning acquisition and use of computer systems, the maintenance of computer hardware is an important consideration. Typically, in large installations, maintenance contracts have a cost on the order of 10% of yearly leasing costs. In the case of minicomputers, monthly maintenance costs are a relatively higher percentage, and maintenance is less often purchased through a maintenance contract. In addition to maintenance costs, the economic consequences of down time, when the computer system is inoperative, must be considered and can be serious.

Currently, manufacturer-provided maintenance and in-house service are the two major approaches to computer maintenance. Yet the demand for cheaper and faster service has brought in a host of third party maintenance companies (currently some 40 companies in the U.S.) with sales totalling $160 million in 1972 and possibly exploding to $2.4 billion by 1980 [30].

HARDWARE DECISIONS

A number of questions arise in determining how to computerize a function or operation. While some of these decisions concern the hardware, and will be discussed in this section, other decisions concern the software, and will be discussed extensively in Chapter III. In general, neither of these kinds of questions can be considered independently of the others.

What Kind and Size of Computer

In most water resources applications the question, What kind of computer?, can be answered readily; usually the answer is digital. The digital computer is much more versatile and hence can meet most of the needs presented by the broad spectrum of water resources problems. However, many problems related to modeling and simulation, as well as some control operations, are most efficiently performed on analog or hybrid computers. For instance, analog computers are being used by the Bureau of Reclamation to control governors, voltage regulators, etc.—"functions that cannot be performed as efficiently or effectively on a digital computer" [31]. Thus, to control certain operations of the power plants along the Grand Coulee, it was recently decided to use 10 to 20 analog computers.

Once the decision has been made as to the basic type of computer, the size of the computational installation (in terms of capability, capacity, etc.) must be determined. The decision obviously depends on numerous factors. Some of these are very subjective and depend on the preferences and the experiences of the user. Other factors are technical or economic in nature, for instance the lack of control and reduced man-machine interaction of larger systems versus their increased capabilities and speed. The result of these decisions can range from a dedicated minicomputer controlling parts of a substation along the California Aqueduct to the huge central computer installation at the U.S. Geological Survey.

A rational decision must consider the:

- Current and projected utilization statistics
- Type and nature of programs encountered
- Number and experience of the computer users
- Modes of interaction with the computer
- Programming and operational staff requirements
- Communications and maintenance costs
- Other budgetary constraints
- Other factors pertinent to the particular application being considered.

A bibliography on selection and evaluation criteria is given in Appendix 5.

Purchase, Rent, or Build

Several alternatives present themselves in acquiring the computer power necessary to perform a given set of tasks:

- Purchase or lease new
- Purchase or lease used
- Purchase and modify
- Design and have built
- Design and build

The full range of these alternatives is seldom explored thoroughly in water resources applications. Frequently a user, particularly the smaller organization, seems to limit itself to sales contacts with the major manufacturers, and fails to contemplate purchasing analyses that, although cumbersome, may lead to more economical alternatives. Providing assistance of this kind to the computer user in water resources could become a valuable ancillary service of one of the centralized organizations discussed in the next chapter. A government organization that currently provides assistance in this matter to other government organizations in the United States is the Automated Data and Telecommunications Service (ADTS) of the General Services Administration (GSA).

The purchase or lease of a new computer has many advantages: often sales representatives give extensive aid in defining system requirements; installation may take only a day or two; extensive system support is generally available. There are, however, disadvantages also: the system may have production "bugs" in it; the price is greater than that of a used computer; delivery, at times a very serious problem, may take several months to several years, depending upon the demand for a particular model. A new computer is often leased, rather than purchased, with a monthly lease price based on 40 to 50 months, and varying somewhat with the manufacturer. These hardware costs are well-tabulated in various sources [32], [33]. Typical monthly rentals for several systems with disc and tape support are shown in table 2-1; the variance in rental costs for systems of comparable speed and capabilities is small.

The purchase or lease of a used computer is becoming increasingly feasible because there is a growing number of used computers being sold for a variety of reasons; the user may be upgrading his line, the machines may be demonstration models, etc. Other factors being equal, a machine purchased locally offers the buyer the advantage of maintenance personnel who may know its idiosyncracies. Service is generally available on newer machines, but the buyer still must perform extensive operational checkouts and assure himself that critical spare parts are available. The advantages of buying a used computer include, in addition to the obvious one of a lower expenditure, the possession of a machine that hopefully has all production "bugs" removed and that may well have an extensive software library that

Table 2-1

Approximate rental costs for several large digital computer systems
with magnetic tape and disc support [34]

Computer system		Monthly rental ($)		
BURR	B 3500/4700	5,000	—	60,000
	B 5700/6700	20,000	—	150,000
CDC	3100	8,000	—	20,000
	3300	18,000	—	30,000
	6400	35,000	—	60,000
	6600	46,000	—	90,000
IBM	360/40	7,000	—	24,000
	360/50	15,000	—	32,000
	360/65	18,000	—	40,000
	370/155	24,000	—	80,000
UNIVAC	U1108	26,000	—	45,000

has been tested and is operational. The software may be tailored for specific peripheral equipment, which may also be for sale at considerable savings. The direct savings in used computers and peripheral devices are exemplified in table 2-2, which is based on current sales literature.

The disadvantages of purchasing or leasing a used computer are obvious. The situation is somewhat analogous to buying a used car; the machine may have been extensively modified and be hard to service, may be hopelessly obsolete, and may not be compatible with newer software and hardware.

To purchase a new or used computer and modify it is another method of acquiring a computer installation tailored to specific requirements. Modifications can be loosely grouped into two types: 1) modifications to the processor or memory, and 2) modifications for special I/O devices. Modifications of the first type are delicate and should in general be undertaken with great caution because processors and memories have very critical timing relationships, and any modification can effect a great number of other operations. The modifications leave the computer in a special configuration that may also present great problems in terms of maintenance, expansion, resale, etc.

Modifications of the second type are quite common, especially on the under $100,000 computers. Incorporating digital-to-analog and analog-to-digital converters, digital controllers, and sensors can often be readily accomplished by using available I/O channels on the computer. The modifications can be done "in-house", by the computer manufacturer, or by

Table 2-2

Costs of new and used digital computers
(based in part on data from [35])

Component		New cost (dollars)	Used cost (dollars)	Used cost: percentage of original cost
Computers+	Large	965,000	525,000	54%
		463,000*	245,000	53%
		383,000	75,000	20%
	Medium	173,000*	95,000	55%
		120,000*	40,000	33%
		157,000*	50,000	32%
	Small	62,000	19,000	31%
		53,000	25,000	47%
Peripherals	Disc	6,000	2,450	41%
		32,500	15,000	46%
	Tape	12,000	5,500	46%
		2,350	1,400	60%
	Core	5,500	3,500	64%
		12,600	7,000	56%
	Printer	48,500	24,000	49%

+Manufacturers include Burroughs, IBM, DEC, Honeywell, etc.
*Our calculations based on data from [33].

a variety of independent electronics houses. For computers over $100,000, generally a "hands off" policy is advisable, so these modifications are usually accomplished by making the special device relate to the computer in exactly the same terms as one of the manufacturer's standard devices. For example, an optical scanner replacing a standard card reader must "look" to the computer exactly like the standard card readers. In any case, the suggested modifications should be discussed with a manufacturer's representative to insure that the maintenance contract, etc. will not be violated.

To design and have built is an option open to any agency with an appropriate staff, which can completely design its own computer and then have it built. For larger systems this is not a desirable approach, because generally a great deal of effort and time must be expended by the agency staff, which has much smaller capabilities than the staff of most manufacturers. Furthermore, most special applications are not so different as to require an ex-novo design of a computer system. For smaller systems, on the other hand, to design and have built is now a distinct possibility, greatly enhanced by the availability of increasingly powerful and inexpensive integrated circuits.

To design and build in-house involves the same considerations. An added note of caution is the difficulty of the production process, as exemplified by the early difficulties encountered by the U.S. Geological Survey in building even a simple special-purpose computer (see Chapter V). In general, except possibly for the smallest computers, design and construction should be left to the professional.

Financial Considerations

Although computers are rented or leased perhaps more often than any other type of capital equipment, there are both major advantages and disadvantages to this arrangement that should not be overlooked:

- The rapid obsolescence caused by advances in technology is proportionately less expensive on rented equipment
- Third party leasing companies can rent equipment at rates lower than the manufacturer because they relocate outgrown equipment
- Third generation software and hardware may remain efficient much longer than their predecessors, thus favoring purchasing
- It may take several years to achieve the efficient operation of a computer installation; it is often unproductive to lease for a short time.

The decisions concerning purchase versus rent remain quite complex and are not readily solvable. The last two considerations outlined have led the U.S. Government to adopt "a general policy of increasing the proportion of purchased machines in the United States" [36].

Time-Sharing

Organizations that cannot economically justify owning a computer generally acquire computer capabilities by purchasing time on a computer. Originally this consisted of buying time on a computer located somewhere else and transmitting the input and output by mail or courier. The demand for service of this kind resulted in the establishment of organizations such as Boeing, Computer Systems Corporation (CSC), Information Systems Design

(ISD), McDonnell Automation (MCAUTO), National CSS, Optimum Systems Inc. (OSI), etc., with the primary purpose of selling computer time. Concurrently, remote job entry terminals came into use, consisting typically of a card reader, line printer, communications processor, and modem (modulator-demodulator). With these terminals, the input and output functions could be located at the user facility while the computer is located elsewhere, with communications performed over dial-up or leased commercial communication lines. Many of the service corporations lease and maintain the terminal equipment, with the user paying a monthly fee based on the size, speed, and capabilities of the terminal. Additionally there is a charge for connect time (the time the user is connected to the system) ranging from about $4 to $13 per hour; for CPU time (the amount of time the CPU is utilized) ranging from approximately $54 to $780 per hour; and for storage time (the amount of time the user keeps programs and data stored in the system) in the range of $0.20 to $0.75 per 1000 characters per day. In an attempt to reduce the cost of these services for governmental agencies, the GSA has established large contracts with service organizations (e.g., CSC) and hence offers computer time to agencies at reduced rates (rates at the lower end of the ranges quoted above [37]).

Time-sharing systems have exerted a substantial effect on the water resources field by distributing the economic burden of a large computer. This allows governmental offices (such as the field offices of the U.S. Bureau of Reclamation and of the U.S. Geological Survey), private firms, as well as remote data collection and construction sites, to have convenient access (via a terminal) to large computer facilities. Hydrocomp has shown that large simulation models can be used on the time-sharing systems of computer utilities [38]. Indeed, several utilities, such as CSC, offer as part of their services, hydrologic programs [39]. Access to these computer utilities encourages sophistication; however, it has a somewhat negative effect in that some remote users may lack knowledge of sophisticated programming techniques and so not use the system effectively.

Up-grading a Facility

The up-grading of a computer facility is more of an art than a science and is further complicated in the area of water resources by the great diversity of computer facilities used in this field. When the need for increased computational power arises, the physical up-grading of an existing facility is only one of several alternatives that include [40] :

- Reducing the workload and eliminating marginal operations

- Increasing service bureau utilization
- Establishing "facilities management"
- Duplicating the current system
- Up-grading the system selectively.

Reducing the workload may be the least agreeable solution, though the elimination of marginal programs and a review of operational requirements should always accompany contemplated improvements.

Increasing the work performed by service bureaus, especially well-defined projects requiring little interaction, is usually economical, but it deprives the user of direct control. This makes it possible to expand the workload as needed, e.g., in the period when the old facility has become inadequate and a new one is being contemplated (a solution used in part, for example, by the Bureau of Reclamation). The utilization of service bureaus thus provides a form of "continuous" rather than step-wise computer power.

The establishment of "facilities management" is a process of consolidating the needs of several user groups so as to make effective utilization of a larger computer system possible. The approach is particularly suitable for large organizations, typically governmental, where the needs of several departments can be pooled.

Duplicating the system can usually provide an 80% increase in capabilities (not 100%, because of problems associated with two operating systems and machine rooms) if the necessary equipment is available. A considerable advantage of this approach is that software compatability is almost guaranteed. On the other hand, the new duplicate system may have components (e.g., a CPU) that were not fully utilized in the original configuration and that may even be utilized less in the new one.

The selective up-grading of a system involves the replacement or augmentation of components—such as CPU, memory, or I/O equipment—which have become inadequate. In the case of the CPU, the approach is usually one of replacing the old processor with a newer and faster unit (e.g., a Univac 1108 to replace a Univac 1106) or adding a second processor to the system (e.g., adding an IBM 360/50 to an IBM 360/65). In the case of memory, the up-grading usually occurs through the addition of core and disc storage systems.

COMPUTER SOFTWARE

In a given computational task the hardware can be regarded as a constant, which is acted upon by the programmer through the variable of software—a set of instructions, or program. An understanding of the principles of software design and utilization is essential to the decision-maker and the specialist in water resources because, as we shall discuss in the next chapter, software presents the greatest problems in effective utilization of a computer.

DIGITAL AND ANALOG PROGRAMMING

For the digital computer to perform a task it must be given a logical sequence of instructions that it can follow. Since the basic operation of the processor and the memory elements is binary, the instructions also must be in binary form (machine code). The programming burden that would result if all work had to be accomplished in binary form is eased by an assembly language, characterized by mnemonic instructions such as "add", "sub", etc., that are translated to the correct binary code prior to execution. Programming in assembly language still requires a great deal of effort because the writer must keep track of addresses, operations, indices, etc., but has the advantage of allowing the user to do almost anything with the computer, because its form is very close to the binary form operations take before actual machine execution. On the larger machines assembly language is generally only used when writing frequently used subroutines, etc., because the subroutines can be written more compactly and execution time is thus reduced. On minicomputers and many smaller computers, often the only available language is assembly language, or one very similar in form. This suggests that the complexity of programs developed for these machines should be limited.

The programming task is further eased by the "user" languages which allow the writer to write in a form similar to algebra or English. A compiler (or translator) then transforms this into the necessary binary code (at a price, as the compiler requires a portion of the computer memory). There are some 300 user languages in existence [41], dozens of which may be applicable to a particular situation. FORTRAN, ALGOL, COBOL, PL/I, etc., are only a few of the major ones, each with its own advantages and disadvantages. Software particularly applicable to water resources problems is discussed in Chapter III.

Unlike digital software, *analog software,* consists of an actual, physical wiring of amplifiers in a configuration representative of a system of equations, i.e., the problem. For example, the equation

$$\frac{d^2Y}{dt^2} + a\frac{dY}{dt} - bY(t) = F(t)$$

is rearranged as

$$\frac{d^2Y}{dt^2} = F(t) - a\frac{dY}{dt} + bY(t)$$

and wired (programmed)

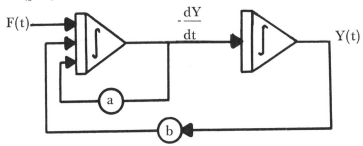

where the triangular symbols represent integrators (amplifiers), and the circles are potentiometers set at the values "a" and "b", respectively.

An operational problem that arises in the analog approach is scaling the equations and then designating and correctly connecting the elements. Generally 30-40 man hours are spent in defining, wiring, and debugging an analog program of moderate complexity. The APSE compiler, the result of research in automatic analog programming, allows direct encoding of the equations and provides a complete wiring list representing the scaled equations [42].

HYBRID PROGRAMMING

Hybrid software consists of a combination of digital and analog programming. The analog portion of the system is wired on an analog computer (generally on a removable "patch panel"), with all inputs and outputs designated. These selected inputs and outputs are wired to D-A (Digital-to-Analog) and A-D (Analog-to-Digital) converters in a control interface (or possibly in the digital or analog computer) and then connected to the digital computer. A digital program is written to manipulate the data, which are bilaterally transferred between the two computers, and to perform the necessary calculations. For example, to evaluate the effect parameter "a" has on Y(t) in the previous equation, the equation would be wired on the analog as shown previously with Y(t) converted and transferred to the digital computer. The essence of the digital portion of the program is shown in fig. 2-7.

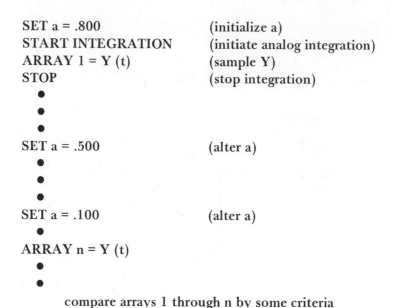

Fig. 2-7. The digital portion of a hybrid program.

SOFTWARE ENGINEERING AND MANAGEMENT

The cost of software production is high. It often exceeds hardware cost by a three to one ratio and is expected to reach the 90% range by 1985 [43]. This suggests the need for a systematic and rational approach to production efforts. At this moment, there is no sufficiently developed body of knowledge to make possible clear-cut decisions regarding the desirability of any particular approach to software production. Thus software engineering and management is only embryonic, and still more of an art than a precise discipline. Some well-established empirical factors that can aid in coping with the problem follow:

- It has been recognized that the variability of a programmer's effectiveness can be very large. A poor programmer may take 25 times as long as a good one to perform a given task. Table 2-3 illustrates the worst/best case comparisons in several areas of software productivity [44], [45].
- The significance of programmer effectiveness is amplified by the fact that the programmer selection tests in use do not provide good correlation with programmer performance.
- During the last decade most engineers have done their own

programming, yet the increasing cost and complexity of large software systems indicates that the specialist may more efficaciously produce this software.

- Programs written in minimal time, though reducing the manpower cost, often require much longer running times; the utilization frequency of a program becomes a relevant factor.

- An index of production costs for a program is the cost per instruction. Developments of basic software, such as PL/I, for computer systems have costs around $50-60 per instruction. Development of programs based on such software has appreciably smaller costs, but data are very scarce. For instance the development of the HYDRO language (see Chapter III) cost approximately $30-35 per instruction.

- The cost of maintaining and updating software is often not considered at the time of production, yet it can be substantial. For some large water resources models, the annual cost may be as much as 20% of the initial cost of the program.

- The cost of producing software involves not only the cost of production; the cost of testing and documentation must also be considered. Cost distribution for the generation of basic software starting from machine code (which may be somewhat infrequent in water resources) is shown in table 2-4. The figures are based primarily on the production of the basic software for the IBM 360 system [45]; the figure of $50-60 per instruction applies to these costs. More significant to a user in water resources is the typical ADP budget shown in table 2-5, associated with the generation and running of applications software.

- The effectiveness of a computer system is a complex parameter to measure, as it is composed of the effectiveness of the hardware, of the basic system software (compiler and user's language), as well as of the ad hoc applications program. (A selected bibliography of evaluation criteria is given in Appendix 5).

- It is impossible to produce large and complex programs that are totally error-free because it is often impossible to verify every possible path through the system.

- To facilitate the composition and debugging of large programs, it is desirable to partition such programs into segment modules of no more than 100-400 instructions, although modules of 10-100 have also been suggested [46].

- Programming efficiency may be increased 20% by the use of "on-line" systems because of the improved response time they offer.
- Program development time is dependent on the computer language utilized.
- Most programming languages are designed to minimize redundancies, a process that makes testing and validation more difficult. Since the largest proportion of effort goes into that testing and validation, it appears that the language emphasis should be shifted to allow for more computer aid in the diagnosis of these errors.
- Programmers must be made aware of the errors most commonly made in programming, and efforts made to incorporate error detection and prevention in compilers.
- Only 9% of the federally-funded computer R&D projects is directed to the software problems customers identified as most agonizing [43].

Table 2-3

Software productivity (adapted from [44], [45])

Performance criterion	Worst/Best
Program size	5/1
Coding time	25/1
Debug time used	26/1
Computer time used	10/1
Running time	15/1

Table 2-4

Percentage of total costs of basic software [45]

Component	Percentage
Design and implementation	30%
Testing and validation	20%
Management, documentation and support	50%

Table 2-5

Typical ADP budget

Component	Percentage
Hardware	25%
Applications software	45%
Systems software	10%
Maintenance and misc.	10%
Operations	10%

SOFTWARE/HARDWARE COMPATIBILITY

Often, the introduction of a high speed, flexible computer product must be viewed as an economic tradeoff between the cost of the device and that of the modifications required to incorporate it. The U.S. Bureau of Reclamation offers some conclusions based upon long and bitter experience in the computer field [47]:

- "From an historical viewpoint, by nature or for reasons of self-protection, hardware vendors deliberately build non-portable and non-adaptable features into their hardware and software."
- "Within a manufacturer's model of computers, there is not always upward and downward portability and adaptability."
- "Portability and adaptability decrease significantly as the size of the program increases. This indicates that modular-type programs are the best investment so that individual modules can be directly interchangeable."
- "Experience in furnishing programs to small consulting firms can be either successful or unsuccessful as far as portability is concerned. For those firms sending a representative to the Bureau's offices for an orientation and in-depth oral discussion on the mechanics of program use, the conversion to a different computer can be expedited."
- "The most successful program interchanges have been with the purely mathematical-type (algorithmic) programs which require little input and output. Many portability problems are caused by incompatibilities in the input/output techniques."

The consequences of inadequate consideration in this area can be very costly. For example, a large data-based system developed for bridge design

BSYS (Bridge System), consisting of 9,000 card statements, had an original cost of $250,000 for development on an IBM 360/40 computer. Its conversion to a CDC 6400 computer cost $50,000, primarily because of a difference in file structuring [48]. This is an example of what seem to be "minor differences" between systems or data organizations, which become a major problem in centralized systems serving a broad segment of users, with computers of various makes and configurations. Another example is UNMES (Utah New Mexico Earthwork System), a system costing $500,000, also developed for an IBM 360/40, which cost $70,000 to convert to a CDC 6400 [48]. By comparison, PROGRS (Progress of Ground Settlement), an algorithmically based program was 1000 times more easily converted to the 6400 [48].

The U.S. Corps of Engineers Hydrologic Engineering Center has also experienced conversion problems, typically in transferring programs from Univac equipment to IBM 360 equipment [49]. Water Resources Engineers (see Chapter I), on the other hand, has not experienced significant costs in converting major programs to Burroughs systems [50]. For example, programs ranging in size from 4,000-8,000 cards and representing about $40,000 each to develop, could be converted in a few man-days, indicating that conversion costs can, in certain cases, become insignificant relative to development costs.

It is likely that the technical problems of transferring software between machines will diminish. However, the educational process that accompanies the transfer will still remain a factor. When transferring a simulation program, especially a large one, training is required in order to learn the nature and restrictions on input, output, and methodology used. Examples of training programs of this kind are the seminars that have been offered by Hydrocomp or HEC.

Considering that approximately half of all the U.S. computer problem-solving capability is owned or leased by the Federal government, it is essential that government agencies with large aggregate buying power continuously press for basic compatibility of the hardware and software among the different manufacturers.

The field of water resources would clearly benefit from such an action. It would also benefit from any action that would bring to bear on the manufacturer the aggregate influence of the significant number of water resources computer users.

SOFTWARE PROTECTION AND PRICING

One of the major problems incurred by independent designers of computer software in hydraulic engineering is the commercial protection and establishment of pricing policies for software. To solve, at least in part, the problem of software protection, some producers are developing "scrambled" compiler programs. In a recent ruling, the U.S. Supreme Court [51] barred software patents. Copyright laws may be more suitable for software protection (as they are for literary or artistic works). Either patents or copyrights, of course, tend to curtail free exchange and distribution, but tend to encourage investment in the production of more sophisticated programs.

In the area of pricing for applied software, three principal concepts are emerging:

- Pricing should be based on the expected return of the software, rather than on its amortization
- In buying software, the user is, in reality, paying for the development of the next system, rather than the present one
- It is difficult to measure the intrinsic effectiveness of software; one can best measure effectiveness through a competitive market.

PROCESSING MODES

Assuming that a water resources problem is suitable for computer solution, the speed at which an answer is required is a key factor in determining an appropriate computer configuration. There are several modes of processing corresponding to the speed at which an answer is desired. Most larger general-purpose computers can be adapted to handle the various modes concurrently, providing the users are aware of the consequences of the resource allocation required for each mode.

REAL TIME PROCESSING

Many forms of process control require almost instantaneous feedback (within seconds or minutes), and thus the computer controlling the process must be available on demand. Real time processing involves acknowledging or handling these problems as they occur in time. The corresponding computer system is generally more expensive because the computer must be ready to service requests the moment they are presented, and generally is turned over exclusively to that job, especially if the process is extremely complex; the other users must suffer the consequences of slow response time for their own programs.

Real time processing is essential in water resources when around-the-clock surveillance is needed, when a system is too complex or widespread, or when the response time of the system is too fast for human monitoring. Examples include turbine and pump operations, locks, and water treatment plants. An erroneous dosage of chemicals in a water treatment plant may have very serious consequences if not detected and acted on immediately; a runaway turbine must be stopped at once, etc. Real time processing can be accomplished on dedicated minicomputers or on large systems, provided that the system can acknowledge "priority interrupts." Further discussion of this type of processing is given in Chapter IV.

NON-REAL TIME PROCESSING

Non-real time processing encompasses many applications and is characterized by a computer doing several jobs "almost" at the same time. Time-sharing, in which several terminals or jobs are being serviced by the computer almost simultaneously, is an example of non-real time processing. A non-real time system operates in much the same fashion as a real time system, but at a slower rate. Unlike real time processing, this mode is applicable when there is no need to sample the inputs, or to provide an output, at a particular instant. For example, a weather forecasting system with various inputs, such as rainfall or wind velocities, must accept or sample these various inputs and then make predictions. The nature of the inputs is such that to receive them within a time frame of 10 to 15 minutes is usually more than adequate, because the predictions or outputs do not vary much within the same time frame (except possibly in emergency conditions such as hurricanes). Other examples of desirable applications of non-real time processing, each with different processing time requirements, are traffic flow on rivers, water distribution, operation of reservoirs and river structures, and hydrometeorologic data processing.

BATCH PROCESSING

Batch processing can be carried out with minimal time restraints, allowing sequential processing when the necessary computer time is available. In batch processing, one job or program is generally completed before the computer begins the next. Programs or jobs are received, stacked, and processed sequentially and the output distributed to the appropriate user. Jobs that are usually carried out through batch processing fall within such areas as research, administration, planning, design, and management forecasts. "Turn-around-time", a term peculiar to batch processing (the time span between job submission and the receipt of the computer solution), is of managerial importance because, though an engineering problem may not require a speedy solution, the interruptions and delays (often hours or days) may greatly decrease the productivity of an engineering staff.

REFERENCES

[1] Hopewell, L., Trends in Data Communications, *Datamation*, 19, 1973, 51.

[2] Piasta, F., Distributed System First of New Breed, *Computer World*, March 29, 1972, 4-5.

[3] Martell, J.F., The Computer Characteristics Review Supplement, *The Computer Display Review*, Keydata Corporation, Watertown, Massachusetts.

[4] Durao, M.J., Finding Happiness in . . . Extended Core, *Datamation*, 17, 1971, 33-34.

[5] Farr, W.W. and Peisel, W.E., An Optimum Disc Organization for a Virtual Memory System, *Computer Design*, 10, 1971, 49-54.

[6] Bell, G. and Newell, A., A Panel Session—Computer Structure—Past, Present and Future, *Proceedings*, Fall Joint Computer Conference, 1971.

[7] Dell, R., Design of a High Density Optical Mass Memory System, *Computer Design*, 10, 1971, 49-53.

[8] Koehler, F., An Impartial Look at Semiconductors, *Datamation*, 17, 1971, 42-46.

[9] Weinberger, A., The Hybrid Associative Memory Concept, *Computer Design*, 10, 1971, 77-85.

[10] Murphy, J.A., Minicomputers, *Modern Data*, June 1971, 60-72.

[11] Hillegas, J.R., The Minicomputer—getting it all together, *Computer Decisions*, 4, 1972, 36-39.

[12] Jurgen, R.K., Minicomputer Applications in the Seventies, *IEEE Spectrum*, 7, 1970, 37-52.

[13] Newport, C.B., Maturing Mini-computers, *Honeywell Computer Journal*, 5, 1971.

[14] Riley, W.B., Minicomputer Networks—A Challenge to Maxicomputers?, *Electronics*, 44, 1971, 60.

[15] Bekey, G.A. and Karplus, W.J., *HYBRID COMPUTATION*, John Wiley & Sons, New York, 1968.

[16] Dracup, J.A. and Vemuri, V., Analysis of Nonlinearities in Ground Water Hydrology: A Hybrid Approach, *Water Resources Research*, 3, 1967, 1047.

[17] Gunther, F.J., Analysis and Implementation of a Compatable Interface for the EAI 693/680 to the IBM 1800, Masters Thesis, University of Illinois at Chicago Circle, (unpublished), 1970.

[18] Davis, S., Selection Criteria for A-D and D-A Converters, *Computer Design*, 11, 1972, 67-79.

[19] Patten, E., personal communications, Analog Division, U.S. Geological Survey, Reston , Va., 1973.

[20] McPherson, M.B. and Radziul, J.B., Water Distribution Design and the McIlroy Network Analyzer, *Journal of the Hydraulics Division*, ASCE, 84, 1958, 1588-1-19.

[21] Otoba, Shibatani and Kwwata, Flood Simulator for the River Kitakami, *Simulation*, 4, 1965, 86-98.

[22] Phillips, R.L., Interactive Mapping for Environmental Systems, Aerospace Engineering Department, University of Michigan, Ann Arbor, Michigan.

[23] Gunther, F.J. and Bugliarello, G., Computer-Instrument Packages and Data Banks in Environmental Data Collection: Some central issues and trends, *Proceedings*, XVth Congress of the International Association for Hydraulic Research, 2, 1973, B39-1-8.

[24] Intel Corporation, Intel MCS-4 Microcomputer System, Intel Corporation, Santa Clara, California, 1973.

[25] Comstar, Comstar Star System 4, Comstar, Inc., Edina, Minnesota, 1972.

[26] *NERC—Corvallis Report, A Guide for Potential Users of Technical Support Services*, National Environmental Research Center, Corvallis, Oregon, 1973, p. 16.

[27] Engle, P., personal communications, Bureau of Reclamation, Denver, Colorado, 1973.

[28] Goldberg, M.C., personal communications, U.S. Geological Survey, Denver, Colorado, 1973.

[29] Glover, R., personal communications, Professor, Iowa Institute of Hydraulic Research, University of Iowa, Iowa City, Iowa, 1973.

[30] Frost & Sullivan Inc., The Computer and Communications Third-Party Maintenance Market, an analysis and forecast report from Frost & Sullivan, Inc., New York, New York, November 1972.

[31] Gish, W., personal communications, Research Engineer, U.S. Bureau of Reclamation, Denver, Colorado, 1973.

[32] Auerback Corporation, *Auerback Standard EDP Reports*, New York, New York, 1973.

[33] Datamation Magazine, Datamation, 1972, EDP Industry Directory, 1972.

[34] Wagner, R.A., personal communications, President, Sigma General Inc., Consultants, John Hancock Center, Chicago, Illinois, 1973.

[35] American Used Computer Corporation, Used Computers, sales literature from American Used Computer Corporation, No. 221, Boston, Massachusetts.

[36] United Nations Department of Economic and Social Affairs, *The Application of Computer Technology for Development*, Publ. No. E. 71. II. A.1, 1971, p. 31.

[37] G.S.A., *General Services Administration Computer Time-Sharing Service*, prepared by G.S.A., Automated Data and Telecommunications Service, Agency Services Coordination Division, Atlanta, Georgia, 1973, p. 7.

[38] Crawford, N.H., personal communications, President, Hydrocomp, Inc., Palo Alto, California, 1973.

[39] C.S.C., *INFONET Library of Applications Programs*, Computer Sciences Corporation, Chicago, Illinois, 1972.

[40] Dorn, P.H., So You've Got To Get A New One, *Datamation*, 19, 1973, 56-62.

[41] Sammet, J.E., Roster of Programming Languages, *Computers and Automation*, 20, 1971, 6-13.

[42] Landauer, J.P., The APSE Compiler, *Scientific Computation Department Report*, Electronic Associates, Inc., West Long Branch, New Jersey, August 20, 1971.

[43] Boehm, B.W., Software and Its Impact: A Quantitative Assessment, *Datamation*, 19, 1973, 49-59.

[44] Schiffman, R.L., Papers Prepared For The Special Workshop on Engineering Software Coordination, Report No. 72-4, University of Colorado, Bolder, Colorado, April 1972, p. 6.

[45] Bemer, R.W., Manageable Software, In: J.T. Tou (Editor), *Software Engineering*, Academic Press, New York, 1970, p. 128.

[46] Myers, G.J., Characteristics of Composite Design, *Datamation*, 19, 1973, 101.

[47] Schiffman, R.L., *Report on the Special Workshop on Engineering Software Coordination*, No. 72-2, University of Colorado, Bolder, Colorado, March 1972, p. 16.

[48] Schiffman, R.L., op. cit. [44], 7-9.

[49] Caruso, P., personal communications, Systems Analyst, Hydrologic Engineering Center, Davis, California, 1973.

[50] Evenson, D., personal communications, Manager, Water Resources Engineers, Walnut Creek, California, 1973.

III. SOFTWARE AND HARDWARE SYSTEMS FOR WATER RESOURCES

For the purposes of this chapter the organizations involved in water resources can be classified in several categories, according to the size of the hydrologic cycle segment (fig. 3-1) with which they are most concerned and also according to their degree of specialization (table 3-1). (In reality, of course, the distinctions may not be as sharp and one may think of intermediate or different categories.)

It is evident from table 3-1 that:

- Computer expertise and facilities increase from the smaller to the larger users
- Larger organizations have operational requirements of increasing complexity
- The scope of the segment of the hydrologic cycle increases from the smaller to the larger organizations
- The size of typical programs increases with the scope of the hydrologic segment, but few programs exceed 10^5 instructions.

A very large amount of data form the inputs to the computational and decision tasks performed at any one organizational level of the table. This is a characteristic not only of the water resources field, but generally of all fields dealing with natural or social environments.

Several pivotal software and hardware needs emerge from these considerations:

1. *Facilitation of the approach to computers,* both for the smaller organizations and for the water resources specialist in the larger organizations. On the aggregate, small organizations are still responsible for a very large portion of the total expenditures in water resources—a situation quite different from other environmental fields, such as meteorology or oceanograpy, where large organizations and larger scale efforts predominate by far. In the large organization, the specialist is frequently limited in his approach to the computer by the very fact—paradoxically—of the existence of a formal programming group or department. Even in the most advanced organization, there is at least a minimum of bureaucratic complexity which usually discourages free access to the larger computer for the less important

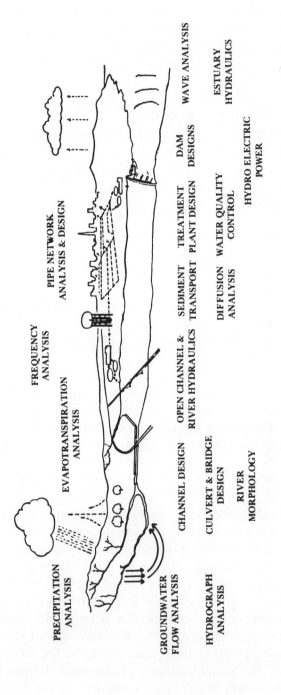

Fig. 3-1. Schematic view of selected components of the water resources cycle and the related technology (adapted from [1]).

Table 3-1

Representative categories of organizations involved in hydrologic analyses (adapted from [2])

Category	Scope of Work	Computer Expertise	Computer Facilities	Program Size (instructions)
Small Generalist Office (e.g., small civil engineering office)	Small component of hydrologic cycle	Usually limited Programmer-engineers	Usually of terminal type	$10^2 - 10^3$
Small Specialist Office (e.g., highway project, drainage project, field station)	Small component of hydrologic cycle	Usually limited Programmer-engineers	Usually of terminal type	$10^2 - 10^3$
Large Generalist or Specialist Office (e.g., large consulting engineer, regional office of national agency or basin authority)	Both large and small components of hydrologic cycle Preliminary planning at basin level Regional operation	Usually programming staff available	Small to medium computer or access to large one	$10^2 - 10^3$
Basin Organization (e.g., river authority, large power company)	Usually basinwide In some instances, multibasin Design Operation	Programming staff	At least one large computer	$10^3 - 10^5$
National Agency (e.g. Corps of Engineers, Bureau of Reclamation, Weather Bureau)	Multibasin, continent-wide In some instances, multicontinental Design Operation	Several programming groups Coordinating and research center	Several computer centers Operational-Interconnections	$10^3 - 10^5$
Global (e.g., some research organizations)	Hydrologic cycle Multicontinental	Programming staff Relatively large portion of staff	Control of or access to large computer facilities	$10^3 - 10^5$

Courtesy of International Business Machines Corporation.

problems—a situation having a subtle influence on the framing and solutions of problems.

These training and organizational difficulties in approaching the computer in both large and small organizations are in no small measure responsible for the considerable extent to which many analyses or designs are still carried out by computerized versions of hand methods which fail to take full advantage of the potential of the computer. The solution lies partly in more responsive software and partly in more easily accessible computer systems, such as minicomputers.

2. *Simplification of the construction of large programs.* In the construction of large programs of the order of 10^5 instructions, which can be expected to occur, for instance, in a fully developed water resources control system, it is advantageous to partition the task by creating a number of "building blocks" that can be easily assembled and manipulated to form the final program [3].

3. *Increased sophistication of computer systems* to more effectively operate water resources systems. The operational problem in a water resources system can be viewed as one of command and control which can be approached basically in one of two ways (fig. 3-2):

- By designing a fully automated command and control system
- By designing a command and control system with man as an integral "on-line" part of the decision and control link.

There is increasing recognition that a fully automated command and control system is inherently both nonresponsive and bound to transmit large amounts of irrelevant information, thus cluttering the channels of the system. Although not publicized, a major failure of a fully automated weather prediction system occurred recently (1972) in the United States. The failure occurred because it was impossible to override the computerized weather prediction system to account for an extremely infrequent event. For approximately 12 hours, during a major storm, the automated system lost contact with the real situation. Dangers of this kind are almost inevitable in a totally automated system, if one considers the myriad of inputs along the river and over the entire surface of the basin to which a control and command system must be responsive if a river system is to be managed effectively. The major reason for the superior effectiveness of a man-machine system over a fully automated one lies in two characteristics of man that only recently have begun to be recognized (in the process of analyzing the great difficulties encountered in developing artificial intelligence systems):

- Tolerance of ambiguity—a characteristic leading to the ability of man to make decisions in situations where an automatic

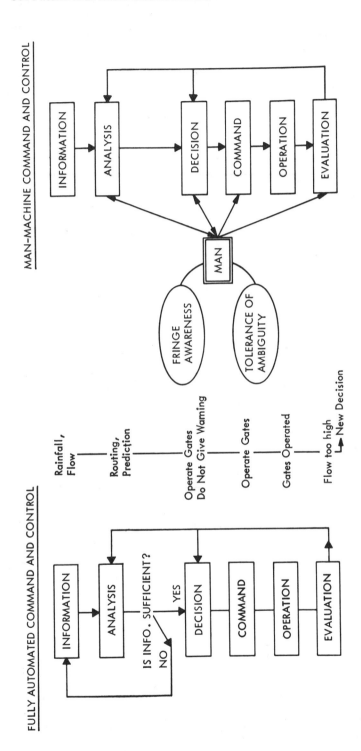

Fig. 3-2. Water resources systems operation—fully automated versus man-machine commands and control [2]. Courtesy of International Business Machines Corporation.

program would either seek additional information or be unable
to proceed

- Awareness of the environment—the presence in man of a large
amount of unstructured and often unconscious information,
which would be prohibitive to collect and analyze in a
computer system. For example, a control scheme relying
exclusively on automatic monitoring of river levels would only
with difficulty and with very sophisticated programming
schemes be able to recognize and act upon special events, such
as a surface rise caused by a sunken barge.

A man-computer command and control loop leads ideally to a water
resources system operated as shown schematically in fig. 3-3. The human
component of the loop consists of "basin managers" and "regional (i.e.
multibasin) managers", who:

- receive information from sources on the river and over the basin
surface
- query such sources for confirmation and further detail
- send commands to installations on the river
- exchange relevant information and send or receive commands.

A command and control scheme of this type requires a flexible
conversational link, in terms of software and hardware, between the
managers and the system as well as between managers at different levels.

4. *Development of documentation methods* to reduce the redundant
programming effort. To this effect unified rules of documentation are
necessary for all areas of water resources. The rules must be flexible so as not
to unduly hamper the program developer, and yet be rigid enough so that a
user is not in constant need of the "latest change".
5. *Establishment of systems for the adequate collection and dissemination
of water resources data.* If the increasing volume of data is to be useful,
systems must be provided to filter and categorize the collected data. The
data also must be readily available to a great variety of users possessing
various types of equipment (as discussed later in this chapter and in the next
one).

SOFTWARE SYSTEMS

PROBLEM-ORIENTED LANGUAGES

The development of computer languages specifically oriented toward the

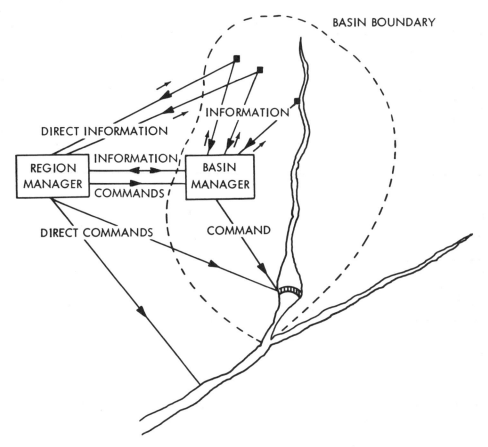

Fig. 3-3.   Control and command in a water resources system [2].
Courtesy of International Business Machines Corporation.

problems and data structure of the water resources field (problem-oriented languages or POLs) is a useful step toward satisfying the first four requirements of the previous section.

A problem-oriented language represents, in a sense, the latest step in the evolution of communications between the user and the digital computer (fig. 3-4). This evolution has increasingly shifted the burden of programming from the user to the language. In a problem-oriented language, each instruction, since it is specific to a particular field, conveys more information, and hence is more synthetic, than an instruction in a so called universal language such as FORTRAN. A problem-oriented language, furthermore, accomplishes all or most of the housekeeping of the program.

An immediately obvious advantage is that a user can learn to program using a POL in his particular field in a very short time—of the order of hours—with little or no knowledge of an alphanumeric language such as

FORTRAN. As will emerge later, this is by no means the only or the most important advantage of a problem-oriented language.

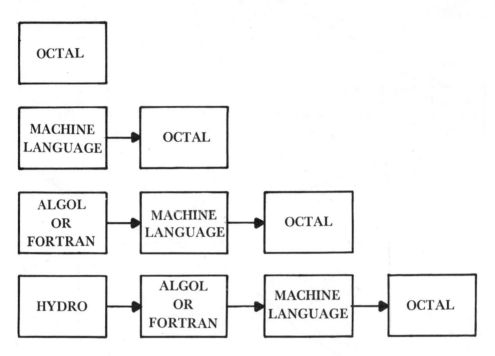

Fig. 3-4. Evolution of user-oriented computer languages [1].

Evolution

The development of problem-oriented computer languages for areas of science and engineering was initiated almost simultaneously in a variety of fields at the beginning of the 60's. The first concept of a computer language for hydraulic engineering was presented at the IAHR meeting in Dubrovnik in 1961 [4] and was implemented in the period 1962-67. By the middle of the past decade, new developments were also initiated, which came to fruition at the end of the decade.

In chronological order, the principal steps of the evolution of problem-oriented languages for water resources have been the development of:

1) the ability to limit the instructions that the user must provide to purely a command and the necessary data. At the same time, the ability to sequentially string the commands, retaining as inputs to subsequent commands the data and results of previous commands [1], [5].

2) the ability to intersperse problem-oriented language commands with commands in a general purpose language (e.g. FORTRAN). This made it possible to write POL programs which were no longer limited to linear strings as in HYDRO, but which now made recursive programs possible [6-8].

3) a system (thus far limited to the area of fluid mechanics) that makes it possible to instruct the computer to carry out complex logical operations [9].

Concurrent with these developments has been the development of libraries of programs that are either used in conjunction with the problem-oriented language and represent the substance to which the language framework is applied, or are used on their own [8], [10].

HYDRO

A first attempt toward building a comprehensive problem-oriented language for water resources was represented by HYDRO—a very simple and unsophisticated pilot language that was designed at the Carnegie Institute of Technology in order to explore concepts and implications and to guide further developments [5-7], [11]. The work on HYDRO was initiated in 1961. Some seven man-years of effort were required to produce the first operational version in 1967.

Like any other problem-oriented language, HYDRO offered, in effect, a greater degree of programming synthesis in its content area (water resources) than a universal alphanumeric language. This was achieved by shifting to the interpreter-compiler of the language the burden of detailed, noncontent-oriented instructions, and by enabling the user to communicate with the computer in the language of the water resources specialist rather than in the general language of the nonspecialist (such as ALGOL or FORTRAN).

The development specifications which guided the design of HYDRO included:

- Much greater simplicity in programming than with FORTRAN or ALGOL
- Commands and data oriented toward the field of water resources
- Coverage of a broad area of water resources problems
- Flexibility to handle different types of problems
- A systematically organized library for stringing programs

- Automatic data transfer between commands
- Availibility to the user of two alternatives in programming a problem involving a string of procedures or a single complex procedure: either to delegate to HYDRO the decision as to what procedure, or portion of a procedure, to go to (on the basis of the range of values assumed by given data variable), or to retain control of the decision-making process. Clearly, the more effective the guidance by the user, the greater the time-saving in the execution of the program. On the other hand, control shifted to the user lengthens the execution time since it increases the probability of errors in the input, or may be less precise, when the decision is based on the scanning and analysis of a large number of data.
- Inputs and outputs by card or teletype
- Gearing of the language to the capabilities (i.e., memory capacities) of a broad range of computers
- Easily designed procedures, easy addition of new procedures to the library, easy removal and substitution of existing procedures
- A modular compiler easy to expand, and easily programmed in small modules suitable for different memory capacities.

Although the portion of the water resources field covered by HYDRO has been limited primarily to hydrology and hydraulics, the language has provided a framework which can be easily expanded to provide a more comprehensive coverage of the field. HYDRO covers five main areas (table 3-2): precipitation analysis, hydrograph analysis, open-channel hydraulics, flood routing, and frequency analysis. The possible flow from procedure to procedure is shown in Appendix 6, which lists actual HYDRO commands. The very descriptive nature of the commands is indicative of how closely HYDRO is geared to the language of the user.

In essence, a HYDRO program consists of:

1. A procedure call (e.g., NORMAL·DISCHARGE)
2. the description of the data, and
3. PROGRAM·END

The data are placed on separate cards from the procedure calls and are inputted in the format:

Variable Name ⟶ data;

where Variable Name represents both numeric and alphanumeric single

Table 3-2

HYDRO Procedures

FREQUENCY ANALYSIS:	*PRECIPITATION ANALYSIS: (Continued)*
TIME SERIES	SLOPES
PARTIAL SERIES	MEAN VELOCITY
FULL SERIES	DISCHARGE
LOW ANNUAL PARTIAL SERIES	NORMAL DISCHARGE
DATA ORDERING	CHANNEL ROUGHNESS
MEAN EVENT	SPECIFIC ENERGY
STANDARD DEVIATION OF EVENTS	PRESSURE FORCE
HISTOGRAM	FRICTION HEAD LOSS
DURATION CURVE	MOMENTUM
HISTOGRAM DURATION CURVE	NORMAL DEPTH
FREQUENCY CURVE	CRITICAL DEPTH
HISTOGRAM FREQUENCY CURVE	SEQUENT DEPTH
STANDARD RECURRENCE INTERVAL	FLOW PROFILES CONTROL PT
GUMBEL RECURRENCE INTERVAL	OPEN CHANNEL FLOW PROFILES
PRECIPITATION ANALYSIS:	*FLOOD ROUTING:*
NORMAL ANNUAL PRECIPITATION	FLOOD ROUT MUSKINGUM
MISSING RAIN STATION AVERAGE	FLOOD ROUT GENERAL
MISSING RAIN NORMAL RATIO	
ARITHMETIC RAINFALL AVERAGE	*HYDROGRAPH ANALYSIS:*
THIESSEN RAINFALL AVERAGE	STD UNITGRAPH MAX INFILT RATE
DOUBLE MASS BREAK CHECK	STD UNITGRAPH VARY INFILT RATE
RAINFALL DOUBLE MASS ANALYSIS	MULTIPLE REGRESSION UNITGRAPH
SIX HOUR MASSCURVES	TRIANGULAR UNITGRAPH
MAXIMUM STATION PRECIPITATION	UNITGRAPH BANK
DEPTH AREA CURVE	SYNTHETIC UNITGRAPH
DEPTH DURATION SINGLE ZONES	S CURVE HYDROGRAPH
DEPTH DURATION COMBINED ZONES	HYDROGRAPH REGRESSION
DEPTH AREA DURATION CURVES	HYDROGRAPH
AVERAGE MANNING N	
MOMENTUM COEFFICIENT	*OPEN CHANNEL HYDRAULICS:*
SECTION ELEMENTS	TOPWIDTHS
AREA ALPHA	CROSS SECTION AREA
AREA BETA	WETTED PERIMETER
AREA CENTDIST	ENERGY COEFFICIENT
AREA HYDRAD AVGMANN	CONVEYANCES
REACH LENGTH	HYDRAULIC RADIUS
REACH SLOPE	CENTROIDAL DISTANCE

variables and arrays. The outputs of one procedure can then be retained as inputs to subsequent ones. Thus, it is possible to write long strings as shown in fig. 3-5. Such a command structure is generally adequate for relatively simple problems, which may be represented as a linear sequence of operations and programmed in HYDRO by a listing of macrocommands.

The dimensions of the components and subcomponents of the original HYDRO system are given in table 3-3. Adding to the dimensions of the

COMMAND 1
·
·
DATA
·
·
COMMAND 2
·
·
·
DATA
·
·
·
PROGRAM. END

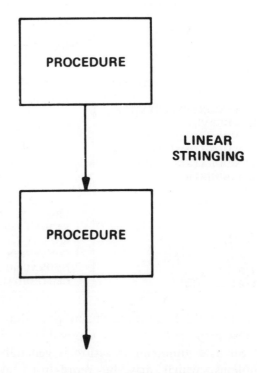

Fig. 3-5.   The structure of HYDRO programs [6].
Courtesy of International Business Machines Corporation.

Table 3-3

Dimensions of the HYDRO System [1]

Compiler in use		Language library	Assembly area	Compiler in storage
Section 1:	650 card images 13000 words to run	4000 card images	4000 card images	3500 card images
Section 2:	600 card images 13000 words to run			
Section 3:	550 card images 9400 words to run			
Section 4:	650 card images 12000 words to run	Note: Largest assembled program run: 1000 card images 12000 words of internal storage to run		
Section 5:	450 card images 8000 words to run			
Section 6:	500 card images 9200 words to run			
Section 7:	100 card images 2000 words to run			

HYDRO software components, the memory required for normal housekeeping in the computer, and the memory for the execution of the ALGOL language, a total of approximately 32,000 words of core memory were needed for implementing the system. However, the system could be broken into smaller segments and thus made suitable for smaller machines.

HYDRALGOL

Many problems in water resources possess a logical structure which is not amenable to a solution by linearly stringing macrocommands, but rather involve complex interactions between components of the problem. Thus, a system of logical commands is required with which these nonlinear problems may be synthesized. Since an algebraic computer language such as ALGOL has the needed logical command structure, a combination of the features of HYDRO and ALGOL was achieved to form a new language, HYDRALGOL (fig. 3-6). The HYDRO procedure commands are identical in format to parameterless ALGOL procedure calls and are used in the same manner. The HYDRO data format is unchanged. Thus, the capabilities of HYDRO are all retained, and the capabilities of ALGOL's logical structure are added in any amount desirable, allowing the user to program according to his ability, from a mere listing of procedures and data, to the full power of ALGOL statements used in conjunction with procedure calls.

Fig. 3-6.   HYDRALGOL = HYDRO + ALGOL [6].
Courtesy of International Business Machines Corporation.

A characteristic use of HYDRALGOL is illustrated by the simple example in fig. 3-7a. A HYDRO command computes a quantity, for example dischage Q, which is retained and stored by the program. A second command requires the stored quantity as input. A linkage between the two operations is not possible if the quantity, although physically the same, is a function of different variables in the two programs (i.e., if one tries to load a variable $Q[I, J]$ into $Q[E]$). The problem arises because HYDRO procedures are not designed for iterations on various quantities (the commands are not fundamental core procedures but rather tasks).

In HYDRALGOL there are two alternatives. The first would be to program a buffer in ALGOL between the two HYDRO procedures, as shown in fig. 3-7b. The second would be to store the core procedures in the user's library and let the user do the looping externally, as shown in fig. 3-7c. In this case, the user would be required to define some of his global variables, especially when there is retained output.

The usefulness of the features of HYDRALGOL becomes particularly evident in the synthesis of a complex simulation model, such as the Stanford Watershed Model IV [12] (see Chapter V), a partial HYDRALGOL version of which is shown in fig. 3-8. In the model, ALGOL statements establish time loops, etc., while HYDRO core procedures perform the simulation of the discrete physical phenomena. The essence of the watershed model is contained in the hour loop, where the code has been reduced mainly to procedure calls. Thus, it is clearly a simple matter to represent the model with the new language.

Since the Stanford Model is a simulation program, it may be desirable to change its structure or to alter certain phases of its operations. In HYDRALGOL, alterations can be made in a number of ways. The overall

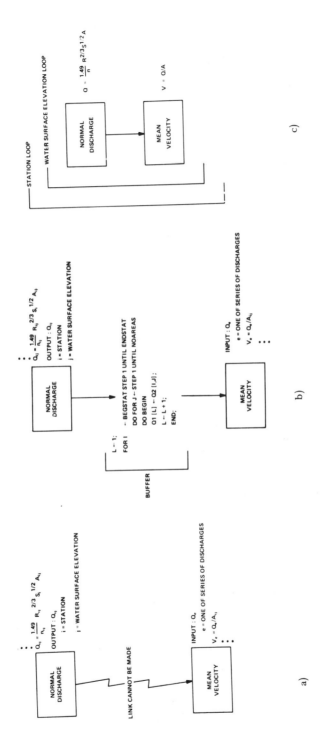

Fig. 3-7. A HYDRALGOL example; a) the linkage problem in HYDRO, b) a buffering solution in HYDRALGOL, c) a looping solution in HYDRALGOL [6]. Courtesy of International Business Machines Corporation.

●
●

A   For FLOWPOINT   1 step 1 until NFLPTS do begin   Flowpoint Loop
●
●

A   For YEAR   STARTYEAR step 1 until ENDYEAR do begin   Year Loop
●

H   EVAPORATION.READ.IN;
●

A   For Segment   1 step 1 until SEG do begin   Segment Loop
●
●

H   READ.PRECIP.DATA;
●

A   For DAY   STARTDAY step 1 until ENDDAY do begin   Day Loop
●

A   For HOUR   1 step 1 until 24 do begin   Hour Loop
●

A   For SUBHOUR   1 step 1 until 4 do begin   Subhour Loop
●

A   Switch S1   L2,L3,L4;
●

H   INTERCEPTION;
●

A   Go to S1 [C1];
●

A+H   L2:LOWER.ZONE.AND.GW.INFILTRATION;
H   OVERLAND.FLOW;
H   GWS.AND.LZS.INFLOW;
A+H   L3:INTERFLOW;
A+H   L4:GROUNDWATER.FLOW;
●

A   end;
●

H   TRANSLATION.IN.TIME;
H   MAX.RUNOFF.AND.RAINFALL;   Output Option
H   EVAPORATION.FROM.INTERCEPTION;
●

A   Go to S2 [C2];
A+H   L80:EVAP.TRAN.FROM.UZS;
A+H   L81:DELAYED.INFILTRATION;
H   EVAP.TRAN.FROM.GWS;
H   EVAP.TRAN.FROM.LZS;
A   NXB   NXB + 1;
H   DETAILED.STORM.ANALYSIS;   Output Option
●

A   end;
●
●

                              Program Continues

A: ALGOL instructions
H: HYDRO instructions

Fig. 3-8. A HYDRALGOL program for the Stanford Watershed Model IV [6].
          Courtesy of International Business Machines Corporation.

structure of the model can be changed by altering the loops, switches, and procedure calls. Individual procedures can be altered by replacing them with an equivalent procedure or by deleting them and substituting ALGOL code. Input and output options can be added to or deleted from the program.

It is important to note that HYDRALGOL, while in many respects similar to ALGOL with a system of library procedures, is still distinctly different. Procedure calls in HYDRALGOL initiate action by the HYDRALGOL compiler to set up global storage for certain variables and to make sure that the routines necessary for the operation of the procedure are in the system. The HYDRALGOL compiler processes ALGOL code, searching for HYDRO procedure calls, which have the same form as ALGOL procedure calls. The HYDRO complier, by contrast, only distinguishes between procedure commands and data variables.

Several other features of a system such as HYDRALGOL are of significance to water resources technology. In the first place, a programmer writing an ALGOL program may utilize any HYDRO procedure as a subroutine simply by inserting the appropriate call and the necessary data. Thus HYDRO *procedures* can be used outside of the area covered by the HYDRO *language*.

Secondly, since all programs in HYDRALGOL are converted to ALGOL, any procedure available to ALGOL can be made available to HYDRALGOL. For instance, the AND, an ALGOL program for creating, altering and destroying files of card images, is available to HYDRALGOL. In a lengthy program such as the Stanford Model, this makes it possbile to store the HYDRALGOL card images on tape and to make any alterations through AND.

Thirdly, generalized POL [8] processors appear feasible, capable of translating the user program and the library segments into the optimal programming language (and thence into machine language) for the computer being used. Suitable adaptation of a generalized processor could be made available to all users in the water resources area regardless of machine type and language, thus allowing complete flexibility, at the discretion of the user, in the positioning of the user/machine interface.

Finally, in virtue of its characteristics, a POL such as HYDRALGOL [13] can be an effective teaching and training aid. The student can build, modify and use a broad range of models from the simplest to the very complex, within the short time necessary to make such an exercise pedagogically meaningful.

FORTRAN-HYDRO

FORTRAN-HYDRO [8], [14] is a POL developed as a teaching aid. The organization of program execution in FORTRAN-HYDRO is shown conceptually in fig. 3-9. A preprocessor is not necessary, because the language is completely integrated with FORTRAN. Thus FORTRAN-HYDRO procedures are similar to FORTRAN IV subroutines. The procedures used in a particular problem are accessed by the normal CALL statement, with input and output effected through a list of formal parameters.

The rationale for FORTRAN-HYDRO stemmed from several considerations [15]:

- FORTRAN is more widely used than ALGOL (especially in the United States)
- Using a standard FORTRAN IV logic, the programs can be fairly large and still remain efficient
- Any existing water resources FORTRAN program can, with some restructuring of data, input, and output formats, be made part of the system
- The elimination of a pre-processor, however, requires the user to have a knowledge of FORTRAN.

A similar approach has been suggested by Smith [16] using ALGOL procedures in lieu of FORTRAN sub-routines as the elementary building blocks to be called upon by the user's ALGOL program. However, Smith's building blocks (now in FORTRAN and substantially augmented) are designed so that input and output of data must be included in the user's program, thus moving the interface between user and computer farther away from the user than in the HYDRO system.

Other Developments

As of now, POL developments have found only limited use in the practice of water resources engineering. Organizations involved in these fields tend, in general, to have their own programs, although some exchange of information occurs within large organizations, as is the case within the U.S. Corps of Engineers.

It is becoming increasingly clear that some organizational structure is necessary to coordinate developments, to provide standards and assistance to the users, particularly the small ones, if problem-oriented languages are to

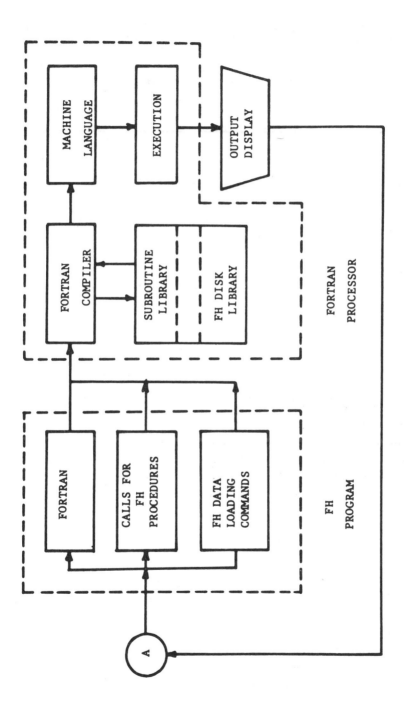

Fig. 3-9. The organization of program execution in FORTRAN-HYDRO [15].

gain wide spread acceptance in water resources. A task committee of the American Society of Civil Engineers, formed with the explicit purpose of determining how a problem-oriented language for hydrology and surface hydraulics could be made more widely available, reported its evaluation of the task in 1972 [15].

In the area of design, the Hydraulic Analysis Branch of the U.S. Waterways Station is computerizing the design procedures contained in their design manual. A program library operates through an executive program to form essentially a sequential problem-oriented language. At present, the language is more rudimentary than HYDRO, as it lacks the ability to retain data from program to program. However, this development appears to be the only one being applied to a broad segment of hydraulic design problems.

Educationally, a POL language—HYDRA—has been under development at Massachussetts Institute of Technology, as part of the ICES system [17].

Within the International Association for Hydraulic Research (IAIIR) a work group in the area of computer languages was authorized in 1969, organized in 1971, and expanded into a Section (Computers in Hydraulics and Water Resources) in 1973. At this moment, there are generally no other national or international organizations that sponsor or support developments in problem-oriented languages or related concepts for water resources.

Two major frontiers need to be conquered if man-computer communications are to reach full effectiveness in water resources technology: the handling of the large masses of data which characterize the area of water resources, and the ability to perform complex logical decisions. While problem-oriented languages can streamline the task of imparting instructions to the computer, they have not yet solved the data problem. A most promising technique for the solution of this problem lies in the use of computer graphics. The results of exploratory work in artificial intelligence techniques in fluid mechanics [18] and the advances in the area of pattern recognition, appear to make the ability to perform complex logical decisions achievable in the near future.

MODULARITY CONCEPTS

The concept of modularity that guided the development of HYDRO will become increasingly important in the generation of software for water resources. As the name suggests, modularity consists of segmenting programs into basic building blocks that can be assembled and tailored to a particular application. Its major advantages are:

- Higher reliability

- Ease of program modification
- Ease of documentation
- Ease of standardization
- Ease of combining modules
- Increased machine to machine transferability
- More efficient use of storage facilities
- Increased flexibility
- Ease of debugging.

Although these advantages are self-evident, the amount of successful modular programming remains minimal at most, and modularized programs are often no better than the monolithic programs they replace [19]. One reason for this failure is that often programs are modularized by arbitrary partitioning. Several guidelines can aid the programmer in developing modular software:

- A module should perform some logical portion of the task—separate calculations, file handling, input/output operations, etc.
- A module should have a single entry and a single exit
- A module should be a "stand alone" component—its operation should be a function only of the inputs and not some predetermined state (thus simplifying testing)
- A module should be limited to about 10-100 instructions
- A module should be a program subroutine.

Adherence to these guidelines can greatly reduce the problems of debugging and of testing which now become limited to that of a small module and its inter-relation with other modules. It can also reduce the often disastrous effects of "minor" changes in input/output formats, file structures, etc. Documentation, another major problem area discussed later in this book, becomes greatly facilitated if modularity concepts are incorporated in all software.

Often modularization is used to edit large programs so they can be run on smaller computer systems. For example, a program to compute water surface profiles for both subcritical and supercritical flow in either prismatic or irregular channels, was adapted to a G.E. 225 computer by linking modules read sequentially from magnetic tape [20]. When this process is used for practical reasons in developing large models (fig. 3-10) [21], it also aids conceptually in understanding the sequence of laws and balances that must be imposed on the system. This is exemplified by the dissolved oxygen system (fig. 3-11) of a dynamic model for predicting variations of conservative and non-conservative parameters in a tropical river system. The model was explicitly designed to be adapted to any river system and to be inserted into a problem-oriented language such as HYDRO [22].

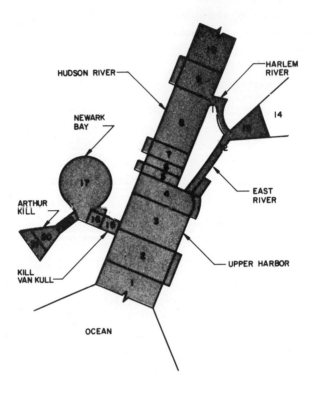

Fig. 3-10. Modularization: New York City's waterways divided into computational segments [21].

PROGRAM LIBRARIES

The development of sophisticated programs tailored to water resources applications logically leads to proposals for the establishment of program libraries. The libraries can greatly reduce duplication of effort, and give the users access to programs at a relatively small cost, compared to the cost of generating and maintaining them. Ideally, library subscribers can receive documentation concerning the programs available, equipment requirements, operating requirements, etc., and can select programs suitable for their needs. The selected programs and pertinent documentation can be transmitted to the subscriber in many ways, including via communications links, magnetic tape, or other means that can directly access the user's computer.

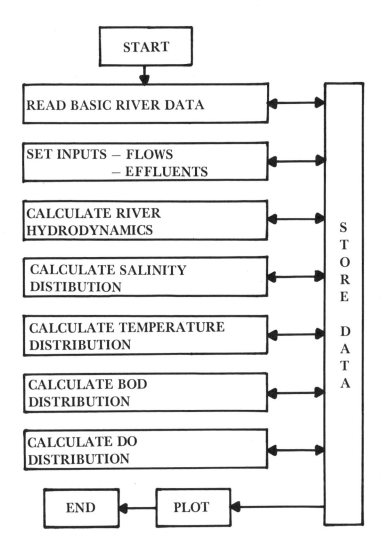

Fig. 3-11.   The modularized flow chart for a DO system [22].

To be effective, library programs should have the following characteristics:

- Adequate documentation
- Adaptability to various computers
- Adaptability to new methods
- Ease of dissemination
- Reliability

One problem in connection with library programs or other "package" programs is that many users will not employ them until they understand in detail how the program solves a particular problem. Often the time expended in such a task approaches the time that would be required if the user writes his own program; hence the user can derive little economic gain from the "package". This problem gives rise to a major question. Should the applications software be written by the user solving a given problem, or should an ADP department be staffed to write them? The user frequently lacks knowledge of up-to-date ADP methods, hence his programs are generally less efficient. On the other hand, if the program is written by an ADP department, problems in communications and understanding usually arise. The best solution is obviously a user intimately knowledgeable in current ADP techniques as well as water resources problems, but this clearly presents training and staffing problems. In the section on centralized activities, where this problem is further discussed, it is suggested that a strong central programming staff may solve this problem.

The ASCE Study

The problem of program libraries specifically oriented to water resources problems has been studied in depth by the Task Committee of the American Society of Civil Engineers mentioned earlier [15], whose report will be quoted at length. Six requirements were identified as essential to any central repository:

1. *Need and Purpose* "The basic need is to achieve both a horizontal expansion of the number of engineers making use of computers and a vertical extension of the individual engineer's capability in computer usage. A central repository has a role to play in this combined education, training, and problem-solving process by providing an information center containing available programs for a specific problem. Such a central source would not only encourage computer use, but offer engineers in need of specific program knowledge the available information regarding their specialty and of the contributors to it. It would also offer them the opportunity to communicate with the central repository or the contributors to it. . . The usefulness of a central repository will depend greatly on the level at which it is established, operated, and financed. . ."

2. *Coordination among user groups.* "The success of a central repository will depend both on the contributions of programs developed by engineers, and the effectiveness of disseminating information upon request. It will take both deposits and withdrawals by a wide range of users to make the system effective and possibly self-supporting. . . Varying degrees of control

regarding results of research and development are practiced by each [kind of user] and the problem of proprietary languages and/or programs necessarily arises. This may not be a problem in actuality but must be considered in determining the operating level for a central repository.

A training program is a necessary element in the coordination phase, in order that effective use of the central repository be achieved. . ."

3. *Level of operation of the central repository.* "The central repository could operate at one of several levels, logically growing from a modest operation to a more comprehensive one.

Level 1. Minimum operation. At this level, the repository would collect and file *abstracts* of programs submitted on standard forms and meeting the standards established by the repository control group. . .

Level 2. Intermediate operation level. Additional responsibility would be assumed for source program listings, flow charts, and full explanation of segments or subroutines of the listing, possibly for publication in a form suitable for copying and dissemination. The proprietory status of the program would require clarification at this stage. Verification would be optional at this level but would be desirable.

Level 3. Advanced operation level. . . .The additional capabilities of providing source or object decks, or alternatively, magnetic tapes or disks, would be added. Programs would be subject to verification and the repository should have access to computer facilities in order to test programs and ensure satisfactory problem solutions. . .

Level 4. Optimum operating level of combined services. Operation flexibility would be incorporated to accommodate programs of four categories:

(i) Programs suitable for incorporation into a library of procedures or subroutines, but not tested by the central repository.

(ii) Programs as for (i) but tested thoroughly by the central repository or a designated associate group.

(iii) Programs written for incorporation into a master "blackbox" system, e.g., a particular problem language, but not tested by the central repository.

(iv) Programs as for (iii) but which are tested thoroughly by the central repository or a designated associate group.

No guarantee would be supplied by the central repository for programs not tested by it (categories (i) and (iii)) whereas a guarantee (but with no legal responsibility attached) would be given with types (ii) and (iv). Once testing, evaluation, and verification of programs in categories (ii) and (iv) are completed and final approval of the repository control group is obtained, a seal of approval could be awarded.

Implementation of this optimum level would require increased availability of computing facilities and highly trained personnel. . ."

4. *Organization and operation structure.* *"Level 1. Minimum operation.*

This level could be operated with a small library staff. The person in charge would need to have some knowledge of computer techniques and programming. The primary tasks would be:

(i) Acknowledge receipt of contributions

(ii) Refer incoming abstracts to review committee

(iii) Catalogue, check and file approved abstracts

(iv) Disseminate abstracts automatically to participating members, and to others upon receipt of request and/or fee, etc.

Level 2. Intermediate level of operation. The competence in computer and programming techniques of the person in charge must be greater, and in the central repository additional cataloging and filing capability would be required.

Level 3. Advanced operating level. The person in charge must have training and experience in computer science with familiarity in the field of hydraulic engineering. Additional storage and retrieving capability for card, tape and disc storage would be required.

Level 4. Optimum operating level of combined services. The person in charge must be a hydraulic engineer who is also a computer specialist familiar with computers, programming, sophisticated languages, etc. Space, facilities, and personnel would be required to provide an additional computer advisory service capability for the easy dissemination of information on file, to revise and update programs, and to coordinate with originial contributors to ensure that revisions or improvements are made."

5. *Location for maximum effectiveness.* "The requirements for location of a central repository include three principal features. First, the location should be easily accessible to engineers by various forms of communication, including telephone, teletype, or by surface or air transportation. Second, it should be a major metropolitan area where engineering meetings are held frequently. Third, it should be close to several types of computer facilities where specialist advisory assistance could be obtained. . . Proximity to major educational facilities would promote educational opportunities and facilitate development work through faculty and graduate students in water resources and hydraulic engineering."

6. *Financing a proposed central repository.* "Sources of funds would include annual dues for participating members, charges for occasional users. . .Additional assistance from . . . other sources would almost certainly be required.

Costs will depend upon the level of operation and might vary from

20,000 to 30,000 dollars annually at Level 1 to 100,000 to 200,000 dollars annually for Level 4."

Examples of Program Libraries

The Hydrologic Engineering Center (HEC) of the U.S. Army Corps of Engineers, which has the mission of developing, disseminating and maintaining programs in hydrologic engineering [23], provides an important example of a program library. HEC has currently (1973) some 30 general programs, written in FORTRAN, that are used in about 50 offices throughout the country [24] (a short discussion of the utilization of several of these programs in the hydrologic problems of California is given by Bennion [25]). The current list of programs includes:

HEC–1, Flood Hydrograph Package
HEC–2, Water Surface Profiles
HEC–3, Reservoir System Analysis
HEC–4, Monthly Streamflow Simulation
Spillway Rating and Flood Routing
Backwater – Any Cross Section
Channel Improvement Sections for Backwater Program
Daily Streamflow Simulation
Unit Hydrograph and Loss Rate Optimization
Suspended Sediment Yield
Deposit of Suspended Sediment in Reservoirs
Basin Rainfall and Snowmelt Computation
Unit Graph and Hydrograph Computation
Streamflow Routing Optimization
Hydrograph Combining and Routing
Reservoir Area–Capacity Table by the Conic Method
Regional Frequency Computation
Spillway Gate Regulation Curve
Balanced Hydrograph
Reservoir Delta Sedimentation
Frequency Statistics of Annual Maximum or Minimum
Flow Volumes
Reservior Yield
Reservoir Temperature Stratification
Interior Drainage Flood Routing
Finite Element Solution of Steady State Potential
Flow Problems
Gradually Varied Unsteady Flow Profiles

Additionally, "a set of FORTRAN callable system library routines for engineering functions are being developed to facilitate the development of programs with a minimum of redundancy" [23]. A current list of pertinent reports and documents is given in Appendix 7.

The Bureau of Reclamation Engineering Computer System (BRECS), which serves only the Bureau, provides a second example of a library of programs, with a broader engineering scope than those of HEC. The categories of programs, the status of selected programs, and the computers and languages for which the programs are suitable are listed in Appendix 8 [26]. The system, now in its fourth year, is quite successful but still has a long way to go toward becoming a Bureau-wide system [27]. The initial low level operation may provide a great deal of experience in establishing larger libraries. The Bureau is also evaluating a very large software package from IBM for terrain analysis. As input, the user provides a data base of information about the terrain to be analyzed. The user can operate on such a data base with parameters describing structures to be placed at certain coordinates, and the computer supplies information about the excavation required for the structures, reservoir volumes, etc. [28].

Thirdly, the GENESYS Center in the United Kingdom provides an example of a worldwide program and service center, offering programs primarily in civil engineering [29]. For a fee (about $250, depending on the particular program, etc.) subscribers may receive a program or run a program at one of the GENESYS Centers. Although the center opened only recently (September 26, 1972) and has at present only a small number of programs (see Appendix 9), its founding principles, as stated by its director, R.J. Allwood [30], offer guidance for the establishment of other program libraries:

- To make use of established professional groups
- To involve potential users at the start of planning of a program, as an effective way of ensuring the actual use of the program
- To develop a comprehensive set of standards covering documentation, computer specification, program issue procedures, and program maintenance procedures, considered essential to the smooth running of the Center
- To verify programs on the basis of agreed and published standards against which programs may be compared
- To consider a policy of infinite portability.

Allwood also states that: "To increase the value of the library, development work may often have to be simply that of merging the better parts of several programs to produce an improved product."

"The identification of software which is to be supported raised the problem of choosing between equal candidates. . ."

". . .the policy that lies behind GENESYS and [the] experience to date has shown that it is possible to gain complete machine independence without suffering many penalties. I know the specter of inefficiency may well be raised, but as you will remember in the late 50's the inefficiency of high level languages was used as the argument for rejecting FORTRAN, etc. I see the 1970's as the period in which we move from FORTRAN to systems such as GENESYS and accept what minor inefficiencies are involved in return for the substantial release of programming effort. . ."

STANDARDIZATION AND DOCUMENTATION

The utility of centralized systems, program libraries, modular programs, centralized data, etc., is directly proportional to their standardization and documentation. (We mean by standardization the establishment of certain guidelines with which a program can be written, rather than a rigid imposition of requirements on every program.) An example of standardization and documentation is that of HYDRO, with its rules for writing programs compatible with the compiler and the other library programs, and with its standardized documentation. However, since HYDRO was intended primarily as a demonstrational rather than operational tool, the reliability of its procedures and the effectiveness of its documentation have not been systematically tested.

To achieve both standardization and documentation a guiding organization is needed to establish policy and provide control. Efforts in this direction are being made by several branches of the U.S. Corps of Engineers (the Hydrologic Engineering Center [HEC] and the Office of the Chief of Engineers [e.g., 31]) for the purpose of "establishing programming and documentation standards and regulations to assist in the portability and adaptability of applications software" [23]. The Hydraulic Analysis Branch of the Corps is also putting considerable effort into documenting programs added to its resident computer. In general, however, there is as yet no clear authority or agreement on the part of national and other agencies as to how to proceed in attacking this problem.

Several major questions must be resolved:

- What programs or elements of a program can and should be standardized?
- How can standards be made flexible and adaptable, and yet not lax?

- Who will insure that the standards are not so restrictive as to hamper innovation?
- Who will enforce the standards, and how?
- Who will modify and update standards?
- How can adequate documentation be provided?

Many of these questions, while essentially organizational, must also be considered from the standpoint of what techniques are available to standardize programs.

Standardization and documentation are of course costly—and their cost is not easily determined. A rough estimate indicates that the cost of providing proper documentation may be 20% of the total cost of a program.

HARDWARE SYSTEMS

CENTRALIZED DATA SYSTEMS

The greatly increasing capability of collecting and processing pertinent data makes it necessary to determine what should and can be utilized. The sophistication of individual components of a data collection system (sensors, data loggers, communications concentrators, etc.) quite often results in component growth more rapid than the rest of the system (centralized files, indices, management controls, etc.). To cope with this problem, overall guidance is needed. Three fundamental questions must be analyzed when considering data acquisition activities if timely, pertinent data are to be available with a minimum of redundancy:

- Who are the collecting groups and what do they collect?
- Who needs the data and what data are required?
- How can the information be communicated?

Some data concerning U.S. Government agencies are given in tables 3-4, 3-5, and 3-6 [32]. The summary of water data acquisition activities (table 3-4) shows that there are 69,260 stations and about 170 agencies reporting. The predominance of the Geological Survey (by more than 10 to 1 in most cases), followed by the Bureau of Reclamation, indicates that a considerable portion of data acquisition activities already occurrs within a somewhat centralized system. By comparison (table 3-5), the agencies interested in water data are quite diverse. Though the table provides qualitative rather than quantitative data, it indicates the spectrum of data users, as well as their particular data interests. The variety of communications modes used in

Table 3-4
Summary of water-data acquisition activities
(adapted from [32])

Agency	Surface water stations	Water quality stations	Ground water stations[1]	Areal invest. misc. activities
Agriculture				
FS	132	46		76
Commerce				
NMFS	18	65		14
NOS	87			2
NWS	878			
Defense				
Army				
CE	1,867	372	712	19
Navy				
NFEC	14	302	168	
MC	7	105		
Interior				
BIA			143	4
BLM	45			2
BR	99	272	[2]4,920	60
BSFW		33		
BM				20
GS	18,095	5,615	18,313	1,226
Ind. agencies				
AEC		614	362	
EPAWPO		[3]630		114
IBWC	149	46		
IJC				1
TVA	133	141	172	61
Federal subtotal	21,524	8,241	24,790	1,671
Non-Federal subtotal	2,322	6,443	4,174	95
Total	23,846	14,684	28,964	1,766
Number of Federal agencies reporting	12	12	7	13
Number of non-Federal agencies reporting	17	159	9	34

Data based on catalog of information of water data, 1970 edition

[1]Active observation wells reported in the 1968 edition of the catalog.

[2]Includes 3,087 observation wells that are represented in the catalog by 285 selected observation wells.

[3]Includes 98 stations reported by Public Health Service.

Table 3-5
Summary of agency water data interests
(adapted from [32])

Agency	Surface water								Ground water		Surface-water quality							Ground-water quality					
	Discharge	Stage	Velocity	Basin param	Use	Physical	Geologic	Hydrologic	Use	Discharge	Lab analysis	Chemical	Biologic	Herbicides	Radio-chem	Pesticides	Physical obs	Chemical	Biological	Herbicides	Radio-chem	Pesticides	Physical obs
Agriculture																							
ARA	X	X	X	X	X	X	X	X	X	X	X	X	X	X		X	X	X					
ERS				X				X				X	X	X	X		X	X	X	X	X	X	X
FS	X	X	X	X	X	X	X	X	X	X	X	X	X	X	X	X		X	X	X	X	X	X
SCS	X	X	X	X	X	X	X	X	X	X	X	X	X	X	X	X	X	X	X	X	X	X	X
Commerce																							
BDC				X																			
NOS		X															X						
NWS	X	X	X	X	X												X						
NMFS												X	X	X		X	X						
Defense																							
CE	X	X	X	X	X	X	X	X	X	X	X	X	X	X	X	X	X	X	X	X		X	X
HEW																							
PHS	X	X	X	X	X	X	X	X	X	X	X	X	X	X	X	X	X	X	X	X	X	X	X
Interior																							
BPA	X	X	X	X	X	X						X					X						
BIA	X	X	X	X	X	X	X	X	X	X	X	X	X	X	X	X	X	X	X	X	X	X	X
BLM	X	X	X	X	X	X	X		X	X		X	X	X			X	X	X	X			X
BM	X		X	X		X		X				X	X					X	X	X			X
BOR	X	X		X	X							X						X					X
BR	X	X		X	X	X	X		X	X	X	X	X	X	X	X	X	X	X	X	X	X	X
SF&W												X	X	X		X	X						
GS	X	X	X	X	X	X	X	X	X	X	X	X	X	X	X	X	X	X	X	X	X	X	X
State																							
DOT																							
FHWA	X	X	X	X	X	X			X			X					X	X					
Ind.																							
Agencies																							
FPC	X	X		X	X							X						X					
TVA	X	X	X	X	X							X	X	X	X	X	X						
WRC	X	X	X	X	X	X	X	X	X	X		X						X					
Non-Fed.																							
N.Y	X	X	X	X	X	X	X		X	X		X	X										
Penn.	X	X	X	X	X	X	X	X	X	X		X	X	X	X	X	X	X	X	X	X	X	

X: Specific interest in term based upon response to Data Handling Work Group questionnaire.

Table 3-6
Method of data communication from site to processing point
(adapted from [32])

	Hand	Tele-commun.	Mail	Verbal (phone)	Other	Point of processing[1] A	B	C	D	E	Remarks
Agriculture											
ARS	X		X			X			X	X	
FS			X					X			
Commerce											
EDS-NODC	X		X			X				X	
NOS			X							X	
NWS		X	X	X	X		X			X	Other-radio.
NMFS	X							X			
Defense											
CE	X	X	X	X	X	X	X	X		X	Other-radio.
HEW											
PHS			X						X		.
Interior											
BPA											Other agencies.
BIA	X					X					
BR	X	X	X	X		X	X				
GS	X	X	X	X		X	X		X	X	
Ind. agencies											
EPA-WPO	X	X	X					X	X	X	
TVA			X			X		X			STORET terminal.
Non-Fed.											
Calif.	X	X	X	X		X	X			X	
N.Y.											Other agencies.
Penn.	X		X						X		

X: Indication of activity (based on response to Work Group questionnaire).
[1]Point of processing: A, Field headquarters; B, District office; Regional office, D, Project office; E. Central headquarters.

transferring data from site to processing point, and the level at which processing occurs, are shown in table 3-6.

A development of growing importance in information management, bound to have substantial impact in water resources technology, is the establishment of centralized data banks (also see Chapter IV). The basic concept is to maintain data at central locations rather than at each user location. This offers several significant advantages over decentralized data storage and maintenance:

- Less costly hardware

- Less costly maintenance and operation
- Less costly updating and collecting
- Improved utility of data-gathering stations
- Less duplication of equipment and effort
- Increased variety of data available to users.

A centralized computer data bank system (fig. 3-12) consists of a group of user computers located at remote sites and sharing a central data bank. The agency controlling the bank system is responsible for collecting data from various data input agencies (many will also be data users), organizing, editing and storing them. Subscribers request data by specifying the type and amount (for example: last month's streamflow data at point "A" and point "B" on the Arkansas River) and receive the data in one of several forms (direct transmission between computers, punched cards, teletype copy, mailed hardcopy, etc.).

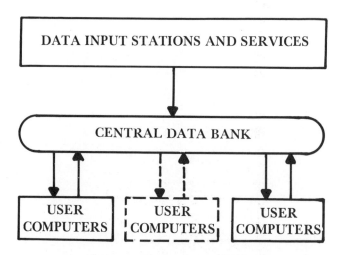

Fig. 3-12. The major elements of a central data bank system.

The control of the data bank system, as well as the questions of retrieval, organization, modes of storage, region of coverage, etc., must be thoroughly studied to optimize the overall efficiency of the system. Specific questions to be considered include:

- Will user computers also serve as data input stations?
- What are the cost and reliability characteristics of the communication network?

- What are the geographical and functional boundaries of a particular bank?
- What data formatting and documentation problems arise?
- Are there constraints on the maximum size of the bank?
- What problems arise when modifications, system updates, and modernization requirements occur?

The problem of retrieval is related to how much additional work is required to condition the raw data received from the bank in order to make them compatible with the user computers. Obviously, this is very much a function of how diverse the user computers are, as well as of the formatting, organization, etc., of the data bank. Many optimum methods of organizing both data and data storage devices (such as discs or core) are available, but each must be analyzed in terms of the specific characteristics of the user computers. Insufficient analysis in this area has been very costly to many users when changing data storage devices and methods. The analysis of tradeoffs in the costs of storage devices, retrieval equipment, and communications is straightforward, usually leading to a per bit storage cost in favor of central banks. A qualitative analysis of the cost of both central and peripheral systems is shown in fig. 3-13, which also indicates the importance of defining the area of coverage.

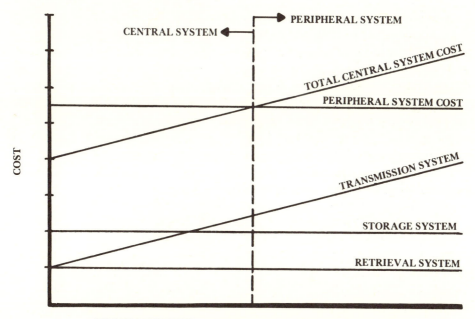

SUM OF DISTANCES OF PERIPHERALS FROM THE DATA BANK

Fig. 3-13.   The structure of the cost of central and peripheral systems.

The needs of the water resources field are bound to be best served by a hierarchical system of national, regional and local banks, as well as possibly international banks or liaison between national banks, each storing data for specific elements of a water resources system. A few examples of possible competencies of the three bank levels are:

Nationwide Banks	Long Range Forecasting and Flood Control
	Interstate River Traffic Control
	Multi-Basin Water Management Data
Regional Banks	River and Lake Water Quality Control
	River and Lake Traffic Control
	Water Supply Systems
	Flood Control
	Soil Conservation
Local Banks	Micro Climatic Reporting
	Local Water Distribution Systems
	Local Water Treatment
	Local Waste Water Treatment

The boundaries and allocation of data among these banks are not likely to be always sharply defined, since many of the areas may overlap. Yet an effective definition can be reached by considering natural and functional boundaries (although communication distances will influence the determination of the area of coverage of each system).

Many users today are reluctant to develop data banks, because of the practical difficulties that have been encountered in numerous instances in retrieving data from the banks. "It is far easier to store than to retrieve" is a frequent complaint. Thus, even where data banks appear to be economically advantageous, their adoption will be a slow process until data retrieval and documentation problems are solved to the satisfaction of all users.

CENTRAL DATA BANK COMMUNICATIONS

Many of the problems of communications within water resources systems exist independently of the computer. The introduction of the computer, especially in centralized configurations, brings with it communications problems that are somewhat distinct. Water resources applications encompass a communications spectrum from two-wire analog signal transmission to satellite communications. Data communications—both to the bank for storage and from the bank to the user—represents the major additional cost (and problem) in a centralized data system. Assuming a somewhat standardized format at each user terminal, this cost is directly proportional to the amount of data transmitted, the speed of transmission (in the sense that line requirements must be specified) and the transmission distance. Three major factors that must be considered when comparing central and peripheral data collection and storage systems are the increasing cost of labor involved in redundant data collection, the constantly decreasing cost of hardware systems (see fig. 3-14), and the increased amount and type of data made available. The U.S. Bureau of Reclamation is currently tending toward large central computer facilities in spite of the communications cost. One reason is that much of their work must be done in underdeveloped areas, where a remote terminal and communication line capability is very important [28].

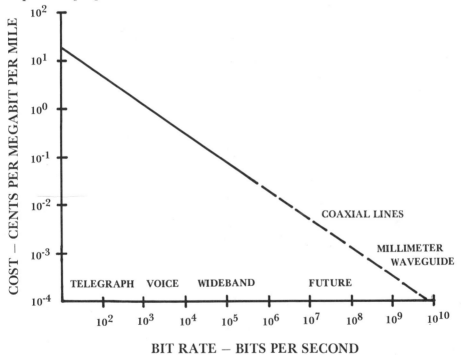

Fig. 3-14. Common carrier network data facilities.

Advances with far reaching influence on communications are those of the satellites, lasers, etc. In addition to their effect on the overall cost of communications, these advances have a specific influence on water resources, as in the case of the Earth Resources Technology Satellites (see Chapter IV).

OTHER COMMUNICATIONS SYSTEMS

The problem of collecting data from remote stations, relaying command and control to stations, etc., are extensive with or without computer intervention. Computer technology becomes a factor in these communication systems when it can elaborate on or speed up certain processes. Rather than just a telephone at the remote site or other end point, an acoustic coupler and some form of terminal become necessary. The methods of communications from remote site to processing point for a cross section of Federal agencies were summarized in table 3-6. Those agencies that perform this task by phone may be readily suited to data terminals, while those that perform the task by mail may, as a first step towards automation, use optically coded cards; the subsequent step would be data terminals. The equipment and technology required in these areas is well documented; applications to water resources are still limited, however.

THE ROLE OF THE MINICOMPUTER

The spectrum of applications of minicomputers in a centralized data system can be very broad; from off-line, stand-alone operation to operation as a satellite in a large computer system. In communications, minicomputers are very efficient in handling the flow of data from numerous input sources and transferring the results to a large computer or system of output devices. As a communications concentrator a minicomputer can poll messages from a large number of interactive I/O devices (CRT, TTY, etc.), assemble the information in a format compatible with the central processor and communications media, and forward the edited information. Relieving the central processor of these message-switching tasks and possibly reducing communications lines results in economic gain and increased system flexibility [33].

Minicomputers combined with a medium-speed I/O communication device provide a very powerful terminal for communication with a centralized system. As we have seen in the previous chapter, when combined with cassette tape systems, minicomputers offer an automatic method of collecting data from an array of data sensors, preprocessing the data, and, when combined with call up devices, automatically transferring data in a batch transfer mode. The nature of remote operation is well stated by Ball [34]: "The very fact that the concentrator is remote from the main computer site means that it frequently operates unattended, in a basement or small equipment room for example. Reliability is obviously an absolute requirement and here the minicomputer is outstanding. Its small number of circuits, all integrated and all digital, give a mean time between failures in excess of a year in many cases. Maintenance, when it is required, is usually rapid due to the small number of circuit boards in the system, and heat dissipation is low so that closely controlled air conditioned enviroments are not required.

"When software changes are needed, for example to improve or alter a class of service performed by the concentrator, it is usual to 'down line load' the new program rather than visit each remote site in turn with a reel of punched paper tape! Down line loading is a special communication mode in which the main computer commands the remote concentrator to consider a message to be an executable program rather than a message to be sent on to a terminal. By this means, the main computer can exercise complete control over all concentrators, the software in each remote location can be updated in minutes instead of days, and recovery from power failure at the remote location is easily accomplished. An extension to the usefulness of down line loading is expected to appear in future remote concentrators as remote diagnosis of faults. Here, if a hardware failure at the remote site is reported to the central computer, a diagnostic program can be down line loaded and the results communicated back to the central site. In this way, the field maintenance engineer could be informed of the cause of the fault before he leaves his office and can then be certain he has the correct replacement parts with him.

"These, then, are the functions of a remote concentrator and the reasons that they are built around minicomputers. As computer-based communications expand, the number of such devices is expected to increase rapidly, due both to their relieving the main computer of significant overhead, and to the rapidly falling prices making them competitive with the more traditional multiplexers. Already, large networks are operating successfully with unattended minicomputer concentrators as nodal points in the system and proving to be a very successful tool in reducing operational costs."

A problem of great importance that must be considered when incorporating minis into a system is standardization. With 60 companies manufacturing 100 different models, this problem may be of great consequence unless the format of data to and from any centralized system is well standarized; otherwise a great deal of computer power is expended in "adapting" the mini to the system. Through standardization, the input/output processing required at the remote terminal can be minimized, thus allowing the mini to be used to run small user programs at the remote site. With the evolution of systems of this configuration, services like the DECUS Program Library for the PDP series computers may provide the user with a great deal of minicomputer software [35]. Furthermore, minicomputer systems have certain advantages that are inherent in systems composed of small blocks. Once the basic operating principles for these distributed computer networks are established, the minicomputer offers additional advantages. For example, systems may be very tolerant of failures because the failure of a single component can be made to have little or no effect on the system. Additionally, developing such a system is fundamentally simpler since it can be built, tested and installed one segment at a time. Employing smaller blocks also makes modifications and expansions easier [36].

OTHER CENTRALIZED ACTIVITIES

Advances in computer languages, modular programming, and other sophisticated programming techniques suggest that redundant software generation should be minimized. The problem of software generation may also be reduced within a centralized organization. The decision as to whether to have software generated by the water resources engineer or the ADP programmer is a problem that has existed for some time, as mentioned earlier. The comments of D.W. Webber of the U.S. Bureau of Reclamation on the software center concept are particularly significant [27]: "The appendix to the [Schiffman] report outlines the function of the software center and briefly describes the staff. Eight members of the staff are classified as programmer/systems analysts and it is stated than an engineering background is not necessary for these individuals. Based on experience, I feel that this would be a mistake. It is extremely difficult for a non-engineer programmer/systems analyst to work on engineering applications because of the communication gap. Another government agency has recently attempted to convert two of our civil engineering applications to a different computer using a non-engineer programmer with considerable programming experience. Only the simpler of the two programs was successfully converted after a considerable investment of computer time and manpower. Although the salaries of the software center staff may be increased through the use of engineer programmers, it would probably be most economical in the long term."

PROGRAM LIBRARIES IN THE CENTRAL SYSTEM

The concept of a centralized data bank provides a useful framework for the establishment of program libraries. Sophisticated water resource programs written in languages tailored to this field can be stored at the bank, and communications links established for the bank can be used to disseminate these programs. Thus, the user can have complete programs, subprograms, routines, etc. transferred to his computer system, and subsequently call in the required data. This has two important consequences. In the first place, it greatly increases the flexibility of the user's operation, while requiring a minimum of programming staff and computer capacity. (Also, many of these programs could be performed at the central bank to filter, condition, or preprocess the data prior to transmission). In the second place, it provides a framework within which minicomputers can become increasingly important and effective components of a computational network (even though many users of data banks are likely to continue to have large systems). It is important to note that in the planning of centralized systems with data banks and program libraries, questions as to the choice and location of equipment, though extremely important, are often overshadowed by questions pertaining to the software system: What language to use, how to format the data, what programs to develop, how to generate the documentation, etc.

NETWORKS

In the area of computer systems, a configuration that may significantly influence future trends, is the computer network—the intimate and sophisticated interconnection of geographically separated computers. In general, networking represents a method of operationally pooling the capabilities of a number of computers; the resultant networks can be classified as:

- Pure Carrier Networks—networks dedicated solely to data communications
- Homogeneous Networks—networks composed of like elements
- Heterogeneous Networks—networks composed of various types of computers
- Limited Access Networks—highly dedicated networks, functionally very limited, exemplified by airline reservation networks
- High Speed Networks—networks suited for handling large volumes of data and batch processing.

The major characteristics of several extant networks are shown in table 3-7. The ARPA (Advanced Research Projects Agency) Network, a hetrogeneous network and probably the most ambitious undertaking in the field,

Table 3-7

The major characteristics of several computer networks
(adapted from [37])

	ARPA	CYBERNET	DCS	MERIT	OCTOPUS	TSS	TUCC
Organization	Distributed	Distributed	Distributed	Distributed	Mixed	Distributed	Central
Composition	Hetero	Hetero	Hetero	Hetero	Hetero	Homo	Homo
Number of nodes	23	36	9	3	10	9	4
Geography of nodes	USA	USA	UC,Irvine	Michigan	LBL	USA	N. Carolina
Machine size	Mixed	Large	Mini	Large	Large	360/67	360
Communication interface machines	Honeywell DDP 516	CDC 3300 PPU	Ring interface	PDP 11	CDC PPU	IBM 2701	IBM 2701
Communication protocol	Message switched	Message switched	Mixed	Message switched	Point to point	Point to point	Point to point
Transmission medium	Leased lines	Leased lines	Twisted pair—coaxial	Telpak	Coaxial	DDD	Telpak
Data rates bps	50,000	100-40,800	2-5 million	2,000	1.5-12 million	2,000 40,800	100-2,400 40,800
Transmission mode	Analog	Analog	Digital	Analog	Digital	Analog	Analog
Message format	Variable length	Fixed length	Variable length	Variable length	Variable length	Varible length	Variable length
Message size	8,095 bits	1,024 characters	900 bits	240 characters	1,208 or 3,780,000 bits	8,192 bits	1,000 bytes

is a network tailored for scientific and research applications [38]. It consists of 34 host computers (November 1972), ranging from a PDP-11 through the Illiac IV with modified Honeywell DDP-516 computers serving as "operators" to link, transfer, and control communications.

The major question raised by the emergence of these networks is what role can they play in water resources? Though it does not currently appear feasible to develop networks specifically for water resources, access to such networks may be advantageous. Furthermore, the success of these networks may lead the Federal government to establish networks for government related work, in which case they may become available.

REFERENCES

[1] Bugliarello, G., McNally, W.D., Gormley, J.T., and Onstott, J.T., Design Philosophy, Specifications, and Implications of 'Hydro' a Pilot Computer Language for Hydrology and Hydraulic Engineering, *Water Resources Research*, 3, 1967, 636-642.

[2] Bugliarello, G., Programming Needs in the Water Resources Field and the Role of a Problem-Oriented Language, *Proceedings*, IBM Scientific Computation Symposium on Environmental Data, November 14-16, 1966.

[3] Daniels, A.E., Some Observations Concerning Large Programming Efforts, AFIPS *Conference Proceedings*, 25, 1964, Spring Joint Computer Conference, Spartan Books (1964), pp. 231-238.

[4] Bugliarello, G., Toward a Computer Language for Hydraulic Engineering," *Proceedings*, Xth General Meeting, International Association for Hydraulic Research, 3, 1961, 12-1-16.

[5] Bugliarello, G., Gormley, J.T., McNally, W.A., and Onstott, J.T., HYDRO, A Computer Language for Water Resources Engineering, *TRANSACTIONS*, ASCE, 132, 1967, 567-568.

[6] Bugliarello, G., and Onstott, J.T., A Progress Report on HYDRO, *Proceedings*, IBM Scientific Computer Symposium on Water and Air Resources Management, October 1967, 179-191.

[7] Bugliarello, G., Onstott, J.T., and Jostes, L.A., The Expansion of the Scope and Role of HYDRO—A Problem-Oriented Language for Water Resources, *Proceedings*, XIIth Congress of the International Association for Hydraulic Research, 1, 1969, A-1-8.

[8] Delleur, J.W. and Toebes, G.H., FORTRAN-HYDRO, *Journal of the Hydraulics Division*, ASCE, 95, 1969, 1993-2012.

[9] Wong, A.K.C. and Bugliarello G., Artificial Intelligence in Continuum Mechanics, *Journal of Engineering Mechanics Division*, ASCE, 6, 1970, 1239-1265.

[10] Smith, A.A., *Civil Engineering and Public Works Review*, April 1967, p. 1.

[11] Bugliarello, G., The Role and Development of the Programming Language "HYDRO" in Hydrology, *Proceedings*, The First International Seminar for Hydrology Professors, University of Illinois, Urbana, Illinois, 1, 1969, 233-264.

[12] Crawford, N.H. and Linsley, R.K., *Digital Simulation in Hydrology: Stanford Watershed Model IV*, Technical Report No. 39, Department of Civil Engineering, Stanford University, July 1966.

[13] UNESCO, *Teaching Aids in Hydrology*, Publ. No. 72-87901. Paris, France, 1972.

[14] Bugliarello, G., Problem-Oriented Languages in Hydraulic Engineering: A Brief Overview of their Evolution, State of the Art and Future, *Proceedings*, XVth Congress of the International Association for Hydraulic Research, 5, 1971, 329-332.

[15] Bugliarello, G., Computer Languages and Program Libraries, *Journal of the Hydraulics Division*, ASCE, 98, 1972, 1243-1253.

[16] Smith, A.A., The Case for a Procedure Library in Water Resources, *Journal of Hydraulic Research*, IAHR, 8, 1970, 89-108.

[17] Roos, D. (Editor), *ICES System: General Description*, MIT Report R67-49, Department of Civil Engineering, 1967.

[18] Wong, A.K.G. and Bugliarello, G., Artificial Intelligence in Fluid Mechanics, 1967 Canadian Congress of Applied Mechanics, 1967.

[19] Cohen, A., Modular Programs: Defining the Module, *Datamation,* 18, 1972, 34-37.

[20] Westall, W.G., A Backwater Program for the G.E. 225 Computer, *Proceedings,*of a Seminar on Computer Applications in Hydrology, Hydrologic Engineering Center, Davis, California, 1971, 1-7.

[21] HYDROSCIENCE INC., Literature from Hydroscience, Inc., Westwood, New Jersey, 1973.

[22] Pomeroy, A.B. and Stark, K.P., Water Quality Simulation in the Tropical River System, a paper presented at the Thermo-Fluids Conferences, the Institute of Engineers, Sydney Australia, December 1972.

[23] 1972 Annual Report, The Hydrologic Engineering Center, Davis, California, 1972.

[24] Caruso, P., personal communications, Systems Analyst, Hydrologic Engineering Center, Davis, California, 1973.

[25] Bennion, R.E., Application of Computer Programs to Hydrologic Programs of the Central Valley of California, *Proceedings,* of a Seminar on Computer Applications in Hydrology, Hydrologic Engineering Center, Davis, California, 1971, 1-13.

[26] Brecs, *Organizational Program Index,* U.S. Bureau of Reclamation, Denver, Colorado, August 1, 1972.

[27] Webber, D.W., Commentary, In R.L. Schiffman *Report on the Special Workshop on Engineering Software Coordination,* Report No. 72-2, University of Colorado Computing Center, Boulder, Colorado, March 1972, p. 67.

[28] Webber, D.W., personal communications, U.S. Bureau of Reclamation, Denver, Colorado, 1973.

[29] The Genesys Center, Newsletter No. 9, University of Technology, Loughborough Leicestershire, United Kingdom, LE 113 TU, October 1972.

[30] Allwood, R.J., Commentary, In R.L. Schiffman, *Report on the Special Workshop on Engineering Software Coordination,* Report No. 72-2, University of Colorado Computing Center, Boulder, Colorado, March 1972, pp. 59-61.

[31] Dept. of the Army, Engineering and Design-Engineering Computer Programs Library Standards and Documentation, ETL 1110-1-45, 9 February 1971.

[32] Federal Interagency Water Data Handling Work Group, *Design Characteristics for a National System to Store, Retrieve and Disseminate Water Data,* U.S. Geological Survey, Washington, D.C., October 1971, 22 pp.

[33] Jurgen, R.K., Minicomputer Applications in the Seventies, *IEEE Spectrum,* 7, 1970, 37-52.

[34] Ball, C.J., Communications and the Minicomputer, *Computer,* 4, 1971, 13-21.

[35] DECUS, *Decus Program Library Catalog,* Digital Equipment Computer Users Society, Maynard, Massachusetts, October 1971.

[36] Newport, C.B., Maturing Mini-Computers, *Honeywell Computer Journal,* 5, 1971.

[37] Farber, D.J., Networks: An Introduction, *Datamation,* 18, 1972, 37.

IV. COMPUTER UTILIZATION AREAS

For the purposes of our analysis, computer utilization in water resources has been segmented into three broad functional areas as indicated by the matrix in fig. 1-1: 1) Data Acquisition and Management, 2) Analysis and Design, and 3) Process Control. This chapter presents the general concepts involved in each of these areas, while specific details and examples are presented in the subsequent chapters on Surface Water, Groundwater, and Utilization. An exception to this format occurs in the area of Data Acquisition and Management, which for methodological reasons will be discussed almost exclusively in this chapter.

DATA ACQUISITION AND MANAGEMENT

A factor exerting a pervasive influence on water resources technology is that the description of a water resources system (as the description of any natural system) requires a vast amount of data. The data acquisition and management needs range from those of a multi-million dollar lake survey (e.g., International Field Year on the Great Lakes, IFYGL) to those of a laboratory sensor. Even if there were no role for the computer in water resources technology other than the collection, analysis, management, and display of data, its effect could still be termed revolutionary.

THE WATER RESOURCES DIVISION — USGS

One of the major examples of computer-oriented data acquisition and management activities is provided by the Water Resources Division (WRD) of the USGS [1], [2], which is the principal Federal water data agency. WRD collects and disseminates about 70% of the water data currently used in the U.S. (fig. 4-1). Surface water data collection includes about 10,000 stream gaging stations and some 1,300 lake and reservoir stations. Surface water quality studies are conducted each year at about 4,100 water quality stations including measurements such as BOD, dissolved solids, specific conductance, pH, trace elements, pesticides, radioactivity, phenols, coliform bacteria, selected major cations and anions, as well as sediment data at 770 locations, and water temperature at 3,200 sites. Daily groundwater level measurements are made in about 2,500 wells, and samples are collected and analyzed from

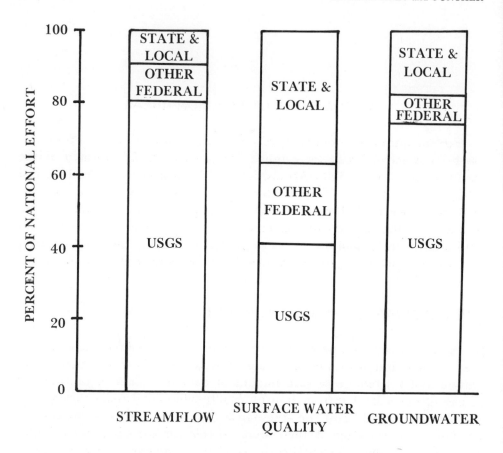

Fig. 4-1.   The U.S. water data collection effort (adapted from [1]).

1,500 groundwater sites each year. About 800 short-term hydrologic studies are conducted annually to provide additional data, including studies of stream regimes and associated changes in stream quality, groundwater studies, water resources inventories by drainage basin or other hydrologic unit, and special studies such as erosion, sedimentation, salt water encroachment in aquifers, and land subsidence from groundwater draft.

Computer facilities (see Chapter I) are used to process, store, retrieve, and statistically analyze this vast amount of data. The current streamflow and water quality records are stored on magnetic discs in the central file for quick access, while historical data are stored on magnetic tape. About 315,000 station years of streamflow data are available. Data representing about 100,000 station years for 50,000 wells and 5,000 water quality stations are also available.

NAWDEX

The National Water Data Exchange (NAWDEX) [2], a system proposed by a Federal interagency work group and investigated by the Planning Research Corporation (PRC) [3], represents a substantial step towards managing the water data of the United States. It aims at forming a confederation of data-acquisition organizations that are willing to make their data available to other users, thus providing access to the large quantities of hydrological data necessary for most water development and management projects. Since the number of organizations collecting water data is estimated in excess of 500 [4], the need for management, standardization, and control is most obvious. Because the bulk of data is collected for mission-oriented purposes, the problem is often not a lack of data, but rather a lack of awareness of their availability. If the data are found in a computer-based file they are often difficult to exchange because of (1) the different types of computers used, (2) data handling software differences, (3) the inability to convert formats, and (4) incompatibilities in storage media.

To solve some of these problems, NAWDEX will use a Systems Central (fig. 4-2) to manage the overall project [5], [6]. Member contributors retain their existing data handling facilities and data files, while Systems Central provides the link to direct data requests. The Central also plans to provide services to convert the data to the requestor's format, provide methods of determining the quality of the data, develop software required to manipulate the data, prepare and maintain a water-data index, as well as provide a data bank for contributors unable to respond to data requests. Although this last function makes NAWDEX a data bank, it is important to realize that its primary function is that of a management and information system and a large-scale central facility is not planned, unless warranted by future activities. The role of the computer in this plan, which will take 4-5 years for full implementation, is not explicitly detailed, but it will be a major one. Computer-based filing, indexing, cross referencing, converting, retrieving, and analyzing are vital to such a system.

STORET – EPA

STORET is an interagency central data bank developed by the Federal Water. Pollution Control Admin. (FWPCA) and administered by the Environmental Protection Agency (EPA). The nationwide bank, centered in Washington, D.C., is used primarily by the Corps of Engineers, EPA, and the Geological Survey (USGS), with some 400 agencies cooperating in data collection [7]. An IBM 370/155 computer from a computer utility,

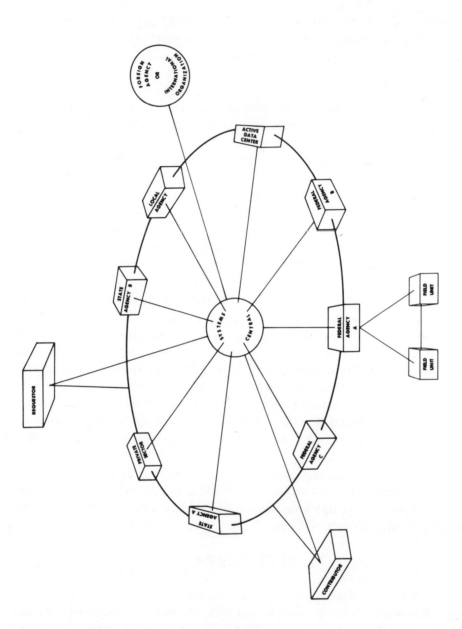

Fig. 4-2. Systems Central and the linkage of units within NAWDEX [5].

Optimum Systems Inc. (OSI), serves as the hub of the system, with STORET occupying 17 of the 60 IBM 3330 Disc Systems [8]. There are two major files, the Water Quality Monitor Data (WQMD) and the General Point Source File (GPSF).

The WQMD file, which occupies 12 disc packs and has an exponential growth that will double in 4-5 months, allows data extraction by geography, parameter, station, date, and by depth. This low overhead file system can support almost any type of terminal connection—or data can be mailed. There are approximately 12 report-generating routines that can be used to process and report the data, including statistics, spatial variations, violations of quality standards (such as BOD), etc. Reports can range in cost from $0.50 to $100, depending on the nature of the request.

The GPSF is a newer file occupying 3 disc packs; its data are derived from permits issued to entities discharging pollution into a water body, and include information on location, amount, and kind of discharge. The growth of the file will level off because the number of permit holders is obviously limited. A small report might typically cost $4-5.

SATELLITE DATA

Satellites for global coverage have greatly increased the capabilities of remotely sensing water resources data [9], [10]; at the same time, however, the satellites present an enormous challenge to our ability to process and utilize the data they are generating. Data can be monitored via satellite and transmitted to earth; photographs can be brought back, and television pictures sent directly to earth. Real time communication from ground-based data stations via satellite relay stations is also possible

Early in 1972, a small unmanned NASA satellite, the ERTS-A (Earth Resources Technology Satellite), was launched by the Department of the Interior as part of the Earth Resources Observation Satellite (EROS) Program. Three components constitute the payload of ERTS-A. First, three television (TV) cameras, each covering a 100 sq. mile area with a ground resolution of 200-300 ft., have the capability of storing or directly transmitting data to ground. Second, a multi-spectral point scanner (MSPS), with four bands in the 0.6 - 1.1 micron range, has the capability of storing or directly transmitting its data. The third component, a data relay system, possesses wide band video tape recorders and interrogates the ground stations. Two types of ground stations are involved: command data acquisition (CDA) stations and conventional hydrologic stations, e.g., stream gaging stations. The primary output of the satellite is pictures—50,000 per year for U.S. data, 250,000 per year for the entire world. The processing of data includes rectification and annotation of TV and MSPS imagery, archival functions, quick reaction functions, dissemination of data, and updating data banks.

As an aid in the collection and dissemination of data, the EROS Data Center in Sioux Falls, South Dakota is operated for the EROS Program to provide access to ERTS imagery, U.S. Geological Survey aerial photography, and NASA aircraft data [10]. The operations at the center, which include data storage, retrieval, reproduction, and dissemination, are quite automated and make extensive utilization of an IBM 360/30 with 65,000 bytes of core storage and 116 million bytes of on-line disc storage. The computer is utilized for data searches, storage, retrieval, and scheduling as well as for generating detailed handling instructions for each request. This aids the requestor, for example, by providing, as part of the shipping manifest, a computer print out of: date, local time, geographic coordinates, print scale, flying height, film, filter, sensor, originating agency, project, role and frame, and order number.

The data gathering ability made possible by the satellite systems is bound to lead to improved hydrologic models and water resources utilization models as well as to the formulation of more global models. For instance, it becomes feasible to develop models to forecast, in real time, water quality for a complex watershed on the basis of data from ground and space stations. In view of the magnitude of the data, data compression and digitation become essential to this task.

Computer picture processing is now a practical real time operation, which involves digitizing the incoming data (received on a microwave link) from CDA stations [11]. The necessary computer programs require a great investment in machine coding to achieve maximum utilization of the computer's speed and memory. New demands for higher resolution, and the introduction of color imagery, will increase data volumes and could possibly saturate today's largest computers. A parallel network computer operation is likely to become necessary. Through these developments, data processing which combines video, infrared, and other data from a multitude of sources becomes possible.

DATA TECHNOLOGY

The technology of data handling generally involves a number of distinct processes (fig. 4-3) in which the computer has come to play or will soon play an essential role:

- Sensing

- Preprocessing
- Transmission
- Information extraction
- Data management.

Computer technology has made possible data sensing with digital instrumentation sensitive to environmental variables, as exemplified by the instruments used by the U.S. Geological Survey (see Chapter II). The role of the computer in preprocessing is more limited at this moment. Yet the computer can perform a number of important functions, from programming data-gathering cycles to monitoring the accuracy and working conditions of the instruments. The transmission of data is usually performed on a real time basis or at selected times; thus the computer can be used to control the timing of transmissions and to incorporate optimum transmission strategies. This capability is desirable, for example, when data samplying is to be performed on an infrequent but programmed basis, in which case the computer both signals the data sensors and activates ("keys") the transmission system. For practicality in the transmission of large amounts of data, preprocessing is generally required. This may involve both digitization (because digital transmission is more efficient, particularly over large distances) and data compression, to either reduce the total time required to transmit large amounts of data, or to transmit only necessary data. In practice, data compression becomes impossible without a computer. Extracting information from the data once they are transmitted and received involves data processing, correlation, statistical analysis, evlauating data quality, pattern recognition, format conversions, and generating missing data. The use of computers and associated displays is essential to each of these processes. Finally, the management of large amounts of data and of complex data collection and processing systems also requires the use of the computer, both as a process control tool and as a tool for planning studies.

Today many data are not being taken, or are taken subject to large errors, because of the cost involved in performing these functions with human operators. As we have discussed in Chapter II, the development of inexpensive minicomputers is the major breakthrough in the creation of computer-instrument packages, which greatly enhance the ability to collect data. This ability to place "processing power" at various points along the path between the sensing and the management functions presents the question, what is the optimum distibution of the processing power; a question which has a different answer for each specific data collection system.

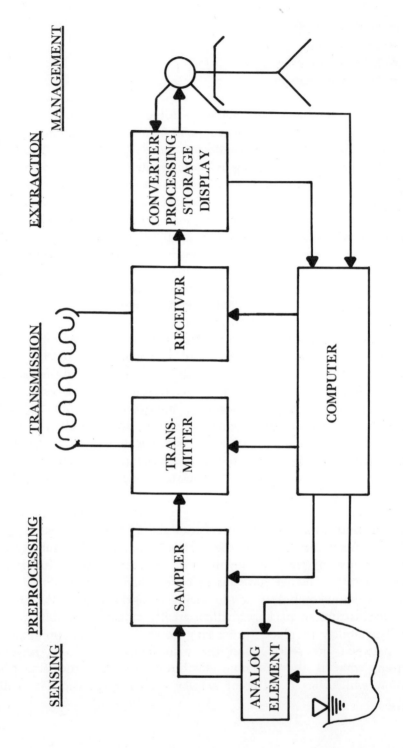

Fig. 4-3.   The computer interacting with the processes of data handling technology.

ANALYSIS AND DESIGN

The analysis and design of water resource systems has undergone a revolution during the past 15 years. There has been a shift in emphasis from the physical aspects of the system, to broader economic and social considerations. Sophisticated optimization techniques have become a major tool of the designer and the analyst, as well as an integral part of the the construction and operation process.

Digital computers have made possible the application of systems analysis to the study of interactions among numerous, complex elements of a water resource system. It is now possible, for instance, to analyze a city's water supply system with some 10^6 connections to houses, a similar number of monthly financial transactions, and 10^7 to 10^8 individual monthly decisions on the use of the resource—decisions conditioned by physical need, life style, supply, etc. A system is generally described in terms of a flow diagram, i.e., a diagram that presents the elements of the system in terms both of their inter-relationships, and of their input-output characteristics. In describing a system with millions of components, the use of graphical representations becomes crucial and the computer, combined with electronic displays, "light pens", etc., offers the possiblity of storing such a multitude of records and images.

The great complexity of most water resource systems makes it necessary for their analysts to focus only on certain elements—on certain input and output characteristics—which come to constitute a model of the system. Thus, there can be many models for the same system; the more comprehensive a model becomes, the more it approaches the real system. The computer offers the means to increase the complexity of a model, but even with powerful computers we are still far from being able to deal with the complexity of most real water resource systems. On the other hand, even if it were possible to approach such a complexity, there would be too much uncessary detail. The crucial factor in modeling is the ability to emphasize, in greater detail and according to need, one aspect or another of the system, or to switch from one representation to another.

Under these conditions, a model of the system can become a most versatile tool. The computer influences the selection of a model and the inputs to it, as well as the form of the outputs. This influence arises from a number of factors:

- The memory capacity of the computer allows many more model dimensions to be considered
- The speed of the computer allows more alternatives to be evaluated

- The complexity of a nonlinear model can be dealt with, yielding more accurate design criteria
- Adverse conditions can easily be simulated, yielding the limits of operational capabilities
- Coupling physical aspects with economic aspects becomes feasible with a considerable level of detail
- Synthetic data can be generated to extend historical data
- The computer offers a much larger range of options for presenting the output. It can be compressed, transformed, printed, stored on tape, inputted to another program or computer, etc. At present, only a few of these options are fully utilized in the analysis of water resource systems. There is a need to place more emphasis on computer graphics and automated interactive design approaches.

In analyzing a system, it is often important to forecast its future behavior. Technological forecasting is not yet refined enough to be incorporated into formal models. Thus, resort must be made to simulations and "scenarios", which are made practical only by the computer. The most difficult aspect of forecasting is the prediction of social trends. Again, the computer has a major role to play in such forecasts, but the chances of failure are high if the use of the computer is not accompanied by extensive knowledge of the social system under consideration. Application of socio-technological forecasts—exemplified by the study of a group at MIT for the Club of Rome [12]—to the field of water resources has been very limited thus far. The bottleneck lies not in the computer, but in the lack of adequate conceptual models and of an ability to forecast social trends and values.

PROCESS CONTROL

Process control can be defined as the totality of actions carried out by man, machine, or a combination of both, to control a given physical process from beginning to end. In a process controlled by a human operator, constant watch is required to monitor the process conditions. When conditions vary from the norm, the operator must make necessary corrections to control the process, e.g., to manipulate switches or levers. Experience is a major factor in distinguishing "good operators", and only experience governs an operator's reaction time and his familiarity with the different situations that may arise within the process. When an unfamiliar situation arises, which requires significant time for its resolution, the result may be an interruption in the process. Furthermore, problems of alertness arise when an operator, watching a condition that may not change for days, months or even years, is required to act rapidly during an abnormal condition.

Computers have greatly enhanced our ability to control very complex systems that could not be effectively monitored and controlled solely by human operators. Through the use of computers, decision-making time is reduced, as is the hazard of human error. Usually, computers also reduce the cost of the control process, by replacing human operators, often a large number of them, with less expensive devices. Other advantages of computerized process control include:

- Encouragement of standardization in the process output, such as a more uniform water quality
- Encouragement of standardized procedures and equipment
- Possibility of more immediate linkage of operations to financial and economic parameters, such as those leading to power demand
- Reduction of the need for excess capacity in the process, and thus, often, reduction of the system size
- Continuous monitoring of safety devices and immediate detection of alarm conditions, such as a runaway turbine.

The design of a computerized process control system involves seeking an optimal combination of personnel, equipment, and computers from the viewpoints of cost and safety. In general the computer can be used either in an "on-line" closed loop, without a need for human intervention, or "off-line" (fig. 4-4). In the "off-line" arrangement the loop is open and all information is fed to the operator, who in turn operates the controls of the loop [13]. In essence, the on-line and off-line arrangements correspond respectively to the left and right sides of fig. 3-2 in Chapter III.

Although the task allocation among personnel, computers, and equipment is strongly influenced by the requirements, variables, and conditions of the particular process, to establish an effective control system several common areas must be analyzed. These include:

- Sensors
- Control Devices
- Communication Systems
- Computers
- System Models.

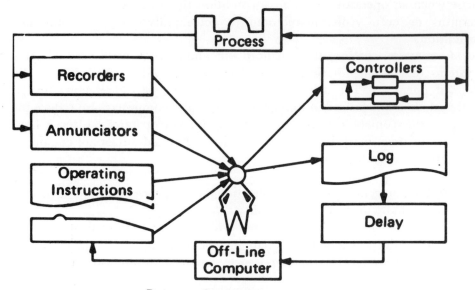

a. Process Operation
Assisted by Off-Line Computer

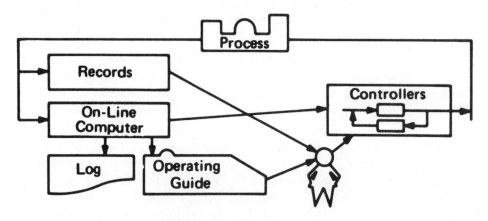

b. Process Operation
Assisted by On-Line Computer

Fig. 4-4.   "Off-line" versus "on-line" computer control [13].

THE ELEMENTS OF A PROCESS CONTROL SYSTEM

In a typical process control system (fig. 4-5), a process control computer is linked to the physical system to be controlled through a series of control/sensor devices that serve to monitor and manipulate the system. The control/sensors may range from simple temperature sensors and pipeline valves to elaborate logic control units that can be linked to each other as well as to the processor. One can recognize several levels of data processing and computational devices in control technology, each characterized by increasing technical refinement:

- Analog devices (not computers) for process monitoring, recording data, and manipulating process controls
- Digital devices for performing similar tasks
- Analog computers to analyze data, make predictions, and control analog devices or directly control the process
- Digital computers to perform the same functions as the analog computers, but with the capability to perform more extensive logical operations and to store information
- Hybrid computers.

The levels, which may all coexist in a sophisticated process control operation, also represent the historical progression toward increased automation.

The addition of an analog device to provide an operator with timely, continuous displays of a system's monitors is the first step beyond manual operations. The initial digital sensing and control devices were merely digital-to-analog (D-A) and analog-to-digital (A-D) converters combined with an analog device. The increased utilization of digital equipment soon led to much more elaborate digital devices.

The next step, made possible by the increasing capabilities of analog computers, is the utilization of these computers to perform real time corrections. Analog signals monitored at selected points of the system are processed on the computer, and controlling signals generated. Digital computers were initially used in process control solely to aid in data analysis and, because of their slow speed and sequential nature, were only used in decision-making that did not require immediate action.

The hybrid approach, a recent development combining all of the above, represents the most powerful approach to process control; the speed and continuous signal handling capabilities of the analog computer are pooled with the accuracy, flexibility, and memory of the digital computer.

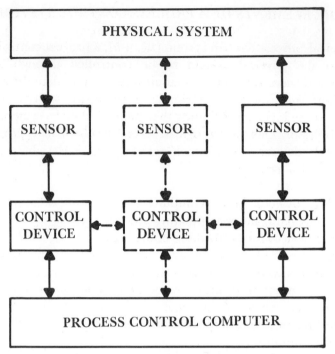

Fig. 4-5. The elements of a computerized process control system.

ANALOG COMPUTER PROCESS CONTROL

Analog computer process control, like any computerized process control, is quicker and more accurate than human control. The analog computer is used in conjunction with automatic control devices, thus greatly reducing operator tedium. This method of process control is best utilized when the number of variables remains small and static, as well as in systems requiring a continuous display of the variables. Unfortunately, when new variables are added to the system, a new component must be physically connected—usually an expensive process, increasing significantly with each new variable added.

DIGITAL COMPUTER PROCESS CONTROL

The digital computer first became employed in the control area as a tool for performing detailed analyses and studying operational trade-offs. If the system has parameters that change during its operation, or if the number of parameters is very large, the digital computer becomes essential. The computer can play an even greater role in direct digital control, which involves direct connection of the computer to the devices controlling the process [14]. Used in this manner, the computer performs a number of tasks:

- Replacement of individual loop controllers
- Direct connection to controlling devices
- Programming of control functions (a task greatly increasing the flexibility of process control)
- Direct adjustment of control actuators to changes in predetermined values.

There are several advantages in selecting direct digital control over analog control methods in process applications. The digital control program is not dependent on analog regulating systems, thereby greatly reducing the cost of installation. The reduction can be directly measured in terms of capital savings per loop, since a direct digital control system can handle a large number of control loops. Digital control also has the advantage of being faster and more reliable than analog control; it has more precision, can better handle emergency situations and control a large number of functions at low cost, and is more flexible in that it requires no equipment changes. Furthermore, digital control is almost essential to feed-forward control—an advanced method of automatic control in which the controlling device operates in parallel with the process (rather than reacting to outputs as in the case of feedback control. Deviations are predicted in advance and control is accomplished before they can materially affect the desired output. The result is smoother operation of the process, more consistent output quality, smaller losses normally due to "out of limit" output, and a genrally more efficient use of the resources—water quantity, power, chemicals, etc.,—involved in the process.

REFERENCES

[1] U.S. Geological Survey, internal communications, received from S. Lang, U.S. Geological Survey, Reston, Va., 1973.

[2] Lang, S.M., personal communications, U.S. Geological Survey, Reston, Va., 1973.

[3] Planning Research Corporation, National Water Data Exchange (NAWDEX) Concept Description, Document No. PRC D-1851.

[4] Lang, S.M. and Doyle, W.W., A National System for Exchange of Water Data, *Bulletin of the International Association of Hydrological Sciences,* 17, 1972.

[5] Federal Interagency Water Data Handling Work Group, *Design Characteristics for a National System to Store, Retrieve and Disseminate Water Data,* U.S. Geological Survey, Washington, D.C., October 1971, 22 pp.

[6]   Doyel, W.W. and Lang, S.M., NAWDEX—A System for Improving Accessibility to Water Data, *Proceedings,* American Water Resources Association Symposium on Watersheds in Transition, Ft. Collins, Colorado, 1972, 91-97.

[7]   Langford, H.R., Personal communications, Chief, Office of Water Data Coordination, U.S. Geological Survey, Washington, D.C., 1972.

[8]   Manning, L., personal communications, Systems Analyst, Office of Air and Water Programs, Environmental Protection Agency, Washington, D.C., 1973.

[9]   Bock, P., Remote Sensing in Space Technology in Hydrology. The Progress of Hydrology, *Proceedings,* First International Seminar for Hydrology Professors, University of Illinois, Urbana, Illinois, 1, 1969, 61-87.

[10]   U.S. Government Printing Office, *The EROS Data Center,* U.S. Dept. of the Interior, Geological Survey, USGS: INF-72-24 (R-1), 1973, 18 pp.

[11]   Bristor, C.L., Callicott, W.M., and Bradford, R.E., Operational Processing of Satellite Cloud Pictures by Computer, *Monthly Weather Review,* 94, 1966, 515-527.

[12]   Behrens, W.W., Meadows, D.H., Meadows, D.L., and Randers, J., *The Limits to Growth,* Universe Books, New York, 1972.

[13]   American Public Works Association, *Feasibility of Computer Control of Wastewater Treatment,* U.S. Governement Printing Office, No. 5501-0145, Washington, D.C., 1970, 77 pp.

[14]   American Public Works Association, Research Foundation, *Public Works Computer Applications,* Results of a Research Project Sponsored by Nineteen Local Government Agencies, August 1970.

V. COMPUTERS IN SURFACE WATER SYSTEMS

Surface water systems probably encompass the broadest spectrum of water resources, from oceans to lakes to rivers to reservoirs to canals. The major activities in this area have been directed toward the control of water quality and quantity, through prediction, planning, design, and management; computers have come to exert a major influence on all of these aspects.

A problem common to most surface water systems is the extensive formulation necessary to describe the systems, as well as the large amount of data necessary to describe the inputs (such as precipitation) and outputs (such as flows or sediment load) of the system. The difficulties in describing the systems and their inputs and outputs are usually compounded because many systems are in effect subsystems, linked to form larger systems, such as an integrated river basin system comprised of reservoirs, rivers, etc. Prior to the advent of digital computers, the data and other information describing the systems could be stored only in written form or in drawings. The computer made possible the storage and manipulation of much larger amounts of information, but the amount of data required to completely describe a comprehensive surface water system can be so large as to defy the capabilities of even the largest computer system. Thus, tradeoffs become necessary between the accuracy of the description (and hence the amount of data stored) and the cost. In many cases, synthetic methods can generate the necessary data, for example, the long series of streamflow data needed by river basin controllers to make optimum decisions on the routing and quantity of flows.

The high rate of streamflow variation makes surface water control especially difficult at the system level. Only short range forecasting can achieve high accuracy; long term forecasting usually becomes very difficult. Yet some form of forecasting is necessary, because of the time lag with which a system can respond to new inputs in order to maintain a desired flow rate at the output points (reservoirs, irrigation channels, pipelines). Often, changes in flow need to be forecast more than a week in advance in order to yield the desired flow to the users.

In essence, these operational problems are of three levels [1] :

109

- Obtaining optimal operation during a short period, such as 24 hours, when all quantities are known
- Obtaining a monthly or yearly policy of optimization when some system parameters such as stream inflow are not known exactly
- Long range planning or reservoir allocation when demands may or may not be known exactly.

At each level, the computer serves to carry out the optimization algorithm and to store and manipulate the pertinent data. Furthermore, when data are unavailable the computer can generate synthetic data series by using, for example, a Monte Carlo approach.

HISTORICAL NOTES

Significant examples of the use of computers in surface water problems occurred as early as the late 50's. For instance, a 1958 paper by Lawler and Druml [2] described the use of a Remington Rand Univac I by the Ohio Division of the U.S. Corps of Engineers to solve the differential equations expressing the fundamental law of unsteady flow, by converting the equations to a system of difference equations. This approach was used to determine the movement of a flood wave in a river channel, at the junction of two tributaries and in a long narrow reservoir (the Kentucky reservoir on the lower Tennessee River, which has a length of 184 miles). The solution for the flood wave in the reservoir is particularly revealing of the performance achievable in 1958 with what for that time was a high speed digital computer representative of its class. The floods of 1948 and 1950 were routed through the reservoir with boundary conditions established at both ends. The solution time (excluding coding time, and time for input, output, and editing) was approximately 12 minutes for each day of routing, or 4 hours for 20 days. The results were generally in satisfactory agreement with observations. Isaacson, Stoker, and Troesch [3], also in 1958, described the use of the Univac I computer for flow problems in rivers. The computer required six and three quarter hours to calculate 13.5 days of flows for a 375 mile stretch of the upper Ohio River. A comparison with the more recent and faster IBM 704 showed the IBM model to be faster by a ratio of 15 to 1.

The greater computational flexibility made possible by the introduction of high speed digital computers was already a very prominent feature in 1958. For instance, local runoff and flow from tributaries were determined without much difficulty, because physical parameters could be changed with ease. However, physical model studies were still felt to be necessary in many cases, e.g., for the flows through turbines or over spillways.

Rockwood [4], again in 1958, described a new streamflow routing technique which was made possible by the digital computer and was implemented on an IBM 650 with a storage drum capacity of 200 ten-digit words. Developed specifically for the Columbia River basin, the technique could provide streamflow forecasting up to 10 days in advance and could also be used for design flood determination or for reservoir studies. A major problem was the synthesis of basin streamflow and streamflow routing through lakes, reservoirs, and channels, in order to establish the flow expected at downstream gate stations. The requirements include: (1) a small time increment to represent fluctuations of the streamflow, typically six hours; (2) a short preparation time for the forecast, less than four hours from receipt of input data; (3) a method for adjusting daily streamflow values depending on input conditions; and (4) a flexible method of incorporating forecast values of input rainfall, snowmelt, or streamflow.

The solution of the storage routing equations on the IBM 650 was accomplished in small successive increments, to combine computer tributary and local inflows occurring successively downstream, so as to yield flow values at all specified gate stations. The storage drum capability made space available for ten day forecasts with values determined four times per day. A five day forecast required 3/4 of an hour, utilizing sixty-eight stream-gaging stations to provide the discharge data.

Utilization of a moderate speed, small size digital computer, a Burroughs E-101, with a magnetic drum capability of one hundred 12-digit words, was reported in 1958, again by Lawler and Druml [2]. This small digital computer assumed a key role in unit hydrograph computations for the Ohio Division of the Corps of Engineers. It could solve in six minutes a problem (including entry of constants and coefficients) which would have required one and one half hours by desk calculator. Other computations found practical for the E-101 were the determination of mean, standard deviation, and coefficient of skew for streamflows, as well as curve fitting to experimental data.

Some of the Bureau of Reclamation's early computer uses were described by Swain and Riesbol [5]. A multiple regression of monthly streamflow, coupled with concurrent precipitation and antecedent moisture, was used to extend the streamflow records needed for a project in Oklahoma. The computer made it possible to select the most consistent estimation equations through an analysis involving 282 correlations. Computations for the 282 equations totaled 7 machine hours at $80 hourly rental, for a total of $560.

Programming and other personnel charges were estimated at $2,500. Although a direct comparison could not be made with manual methods, it was believed that manual methods would have been much more expensive and substantially lower in accuracy.

A most intricate and time-consuming problem of the Bureau of Reclamation has always been the coordinated operational study of systems of multi-purpose reservoirs and power plants. Swain and Riesbol reported that in a study of the Canyon Ferry Reservoirs and Power Plant operation, in order to determine the hydroelectric power production for various conditons, more than 4,500 individual entries were needed to store basic data, and 3,500 separate computer instructions and input values were necessary to complete the study. A flow-duration and sediment-rating curve analysis to establish a reliable estimate of sediment inflow into the Glenn Canyon Reservoir was performed on a digital computer at a cost of $1,500. It was estimated that the same study performed by manual computation would have cost more than $5,000. A further benefit which emerged from the computer study was the ability to keep computations completely up-to-date at a relatively small cost, whereas to update the manual computation would have required an expenditure almost as large as that for the original manual study.

The example emphasizes the early realization of the importance of electronic computation from the viewpoint of the planner. Through the use of the computer the planner acquired the ability, with only slight modifications of a computer program, to compare, for instance, the effects of the removal or relocation of a reservoir or a power plant. As a result *optimal* multi-purpose operation became a reality, rather than the *satisfactory* operation that could be achieved by a manual solution.

Some early uses of digital equipment by the U.S. Geological Survey to analyze and process streamflow data were reported by Harbeck and Isherwood in 1959 [6]. The Geological Survey was described as making full use, at the time, of its general purpose digital computer, a Datatron 205. One-fourth of the available time on the computer was used for hydrologic studies. The work done on the computer was so successful that plans were soon made to extend the capacity of the facility by installing a computer 10 times faster than the Datatron 205. The decision to employ a general purpose digital computer was preceded by an assessment of the types of Geological Survey studies that could be feasible with such a computer. Many years of streamflow data had been accumulated but few analyses had ever been made. In the analysis of daily streamflow, the computations are simple but, as discussed earlier in this chapter, the amount of data is large. The problems encountered involved finding an efficient method of converting the data to a form suitable for direct computer input, and providing a verification procedure for the output. The Geological Survey chose paper tape as the storage medium, primarily because the data (discharge) were single-valued for each daily time period and could be used in a rigorous time sequence. The Datatron 205 could read paper tape, photoelectrically, at high speeds (540 characters per second). With paper tape, inexpensive portable paper punching machines could be used, which allowed data transcription to be accomplished in field offices rather than at the computer in Washington, D.C. Machine computations required approximately 4.5 to 5 minutes. per station-year for the basic analysis.

By 1959, the computer had been used to analyze 30,000 station-years of records. Work had also been done by this time on developing computer methods to process raw streamflow data. Stream stages had been recorded on strip charts, which are essentially analog records. Initially, a special purpose computer was developed to scan a standard strip chart photoelectrically by monitoring the gage height at set intervals. Although such a computer was simple in basic design, many practical complications were encountered, leading to the firm conclusion that special purpose computers were inherently expensive and general purpose computers should be utilized as much as possible.

In recording data on water loss studies, it was decided that hourly averages, which were previously determined graphically in the form of a chart, would be recorded both on the charts and on paper tapes. The field equipment for recording data had three components: (1) an analog-to-digital converter, which converted the position of a potentiometer to a digital equivalent, (2) a programmer, which inserted computer commands and information, and (3) a motorized punch, which perforated the paper tape. Initially it was thought that the Datatron 205 would require two-thirds of its storage capacity for program commands, leaving the remaining third for storage of data—which allowed only a twelve-hour period for data collection. Later the program was found to require less storage space, and hence to allow a longer data collection period.

In 1958 a configuration was developed using three multi-channel potentiometers to record data which were also punched on paper tape. Data from an eight channel recorder was computed on the Datatron 205; this was found to require approximately one hour per one week's data, in comparison to two and a half work days for manual processing.

The progress and benefits the digital computer had produced in the planning and design of major power plants were also described by Grimes and Von Gunten [7] in terms of the Corps of Engineers' experience on the lower Columbia and Snake Rivers. Projects in these areas were units of a slackwater navigation-power development plan. The authors noted that manpower was not reduced but rather shifted when a computer was utilized on a project. Persons skilled in analyzing certain water resource data were generally supplemented or replaced by a staff capable of giving detailed instructions to the digital computer.

On the lower Columbia and lower Snake River projects, the first study to reap significant advantages from the introduction of the computer was the Ice Harbor Lock and Dam. Initial design studies and analyses of the 90 ft. high by 91 ft. wide vertical lift lock which weighs 1,400,000 lbs, were accomplished on the computer. During the project, the computer was also used for operational studies, turbine design, and processing hydrological data. Studies on a power house such as the John Day Project, a 3,000,000 kw operation, demonstrated the cost-benefit studies made possible by the computer: proper correlations of generator, turbine, powerhead, and streamflow characteristics led to savings of $30,000,000 to $50,000,000 over non-computer methods. Approximately 100 programs for an IBM 650 were used in each planning and design stage.

The Goodyear Electronic Differential Analyzer (GEDA), an analog computer procured originally in 1954, was used extensively by the Ohio River Division of the Corps of Engineers for solving flood routing problems [2]. Routing equations were readily solved by the GEDA when expressed in differential form. Input to the computer from a hydrograph was accomplished by means of a curve follower. The analog then continuously computed the rate of change of outflow and displayed it in the form of a continuous hydrograph. Multiple reach routing could be obtained by cascading the stages. By using a convenient time scale of 5 seconds for 1 day, the solution time for a 20 day flood, including the settings of the function generator and the mounting of hydrographs, was approximately 10 minutes. Actual computer running time was 100 seconds, whereas hand calculations, with traditional computing aids, required up to two hours.

A second example of reservoir regulation using the GEDA concerned nine consecutive reaches where information on the effects of the regulation at each reach was desired. The area analyzed covered the 900 miles from Wheeling, West Virginia to Metropolis, Illinois. Total solution time was approximately ten minutes. Actual computer running time for a 40 day flood was 40 seconds, compared to more than 8 hours by conventional methods.

A final example of the use of the GEDA involves severe fluctuations in navigational pools at harbor sites, due to improper power releases made for power generation during peak load periods. The fluctuations were monitored while trial runs were performed with various schedules of release, covering the range normally anticipated. The time savings of the GEDA solution with respect to hand methods was estimated to be approximately 100 to 1.

DATA ACQUISITION AND MANAGEMENT

WATER QUALITY MONITORING

A significant example of data collection technology is the automated monitoring system developed by the New York State Department of Environmental Conservation [8]. The system is operated with a Burroughs B-3500 computer and two software packages, a real time module, and an update and report module. The real time module automatically collects data, checks data limits and the rates of change of the limits, transmits commands to monitors, displays alert and alarm conditions, and provides for human intervention. The update and report module produces status reports and allows for data editing. The remote terminal, an ASR-35 teletypewriter, receives alarm information from the computer. It can also request information directly from the computer or monitors and can transmit commands to the monitors. The addition of new terminals leads to increased capabilities, ranging from backup for monitor interrogation to plotting formal water quality maps, to assistance in the planning, management, and operation of New York's Pure Waters Program.

Basically the system consists of four building blocks: monitors, computer center, remote terminal and telecommunications system. Of a network of 200 active surface water sampling stations, 12 have automated monitors (Technicon CSM-12). The monitors are of major, minor, and satellite types, the first consisting of a sheltered facility capable of digitally transmitting to the computer center data on eight or more parameters. If used in conjunction with an automatic monitor, a computer can:

- Scan the output data at a high rate (every six minutes)
- Activate alarms during a high level condition
- Standardize the analysis for different parameters
- Provide additional monitoring of a particular parameter during a high limit condition
- Activate samplers to obtain additional data for supplementary studies.

The telecommuncations system provides a method for two-way communications in the monitoring system. The equipment can receive and condition signals from sensors in preparation for transmission via acoustic

coupler (Bell System 103A-2). The Department of Environmental Conservation believes this approach to be the most economical one for reliable, long
distance data transmission. The communications system conditions the
environmental parameter signals, functional command signals, and alarm
signals.

Several points emerge from the experience in the development of this
system:

- At the present state of the art, automatic water quality
  monitors should not totally replace manual sampling, but rather
  supplement it where rapid fluctuations are experienced
- A well developed real time computer system procedure must be
  employed for efficient automatic water quality monitoring
- A staff of electronic engineers and technicians is necessary to
  calibrate, operate, and maintain the system
- In any case of automatic monitoring, the reliability of existing
  sensors must be improved (possibly through more research and
  greater cooperation between industry, government, and users).

FLOOD CONTROL DATA

Effective flood control requires timely reception and analysis of a large
amount of data. A successful example of this process is that of the Reservoir
Control Center (RCC) of the New England Division of the U.S. Corps of
Engineers. The Center has combined an IBM 1130 (16K) with the Automatic
Radio Interrogation System (ARIS) built by Motorola [9]. The resulting
system is designed to interrogate, tabulate, and plot hydrologic data during a
flood. Interrogation of each of the 41 ARIS Data Reporting Stations is
initiated by the computer, which receives data on one to four
parameters—for example, tidal stage, precipitation, or river stage—with a total
time lapse of about 3 seconds per station. Some of the interrogation options
available through keyboard selection include:

- Interrogation of any single station
- Interrogation of all stations in a programmed sequence
- Automatic interrogation at selected times.

Additionally, each flood control dam within the system relays to the center
data concerning climatological and hydrological conditions [10].

The output of the interrogation system is handled by ad hoc data
processing and management programs. Some of the data files include

drainage area, alert stage, flood stage, stage-discharge, stage-capacity, plotting
scales, historical readings on each station, as well as long term storage of
stage data. The long term storage is compacted to allow about 4 years data
on one disc. Many of the processing programs are alarm programs that
automatically signal alarm conditions, alter the alarm tolerances, and initiate
more frequent interrogations. These programs include alarms for flood
stages, warning stages, rainfall differential, and nonvalid and missing data.
Routines are also available to plot stage and discharge hydrographs, as well as
pool stage outflow and inflow for the flood control dams.

ADJUSTING RECORDS

Many water resource problems require continuous data records, for
example open channel flow data, which is usually obtained by recording
stream gages at various points along a channel. Although digital recorders are
now rapidly replacing the chart type analog recorders and provide data in a
form readily usable by automated data processors, to fully utilize these
time-saving features algorithms are needed to incorporate "adjustments"
(such as gage height corrections) into the computer programs. Occasionally
inadequate stream data make it necessary to simulate the missing data from
traces of data taken from each of the gaging stations. An example of this is
the multi-variable analysis of Granthan et. al. [11]. Using an auto-regression
program, weekly flows were jointly generated for a number of stations,
based on flows from a previous month. The program consisted of calculating
weekly averages based on historical data, applying a normalizing transform,
programming the transform into a data generator, and applying an inverse
transform to the generated values. Synthesized data generated in this fashion
has been found to be statistically similar to that on record.

Another example is an algorithm developed by Mills and Snyder [12] for
adjusting stream gage records. The algorithm involves editing streamflow
data through sequential application of three data processing programs. The
first program uses missing data as a signal to control selective plotting of the
stage before and after the record break. The second program uses data from
the previous program to insert estimates or to make corrections, and the
third program further refines the corrections.

ANALYSIS AND DESIGN

Once the computer's effectiveness in improving existing computational
methods for surface water systems was demonstrated, new methods were
very rapidly introduced, which owed their existence to the availability of

high speed computers with large memories, as well as to some new forms of computing machinery combining digital and analog components.

DYNAMIC PROGRAMMING AND MONTE CARLO METHODS

As early as 1963, Hall and Howell [13] described a procedure for the optimization of a single purpose reservoir, using a dynamic programming scheme (for a general description of the technique see [14]). The scheme, which used return functions over intervals of time, was coupled with a Monte Carlo technique (for a general description of the technique see [15]), possible in practice only through the use of a digital computer. The scheme selected random inflows from synthetically generated data. It was quickly perceived that a well-planned computer program could eliminate lengthy records from the computer storage area. This was accomplished by selecting short time series from longer series of records in a random fashion, to generate a set of hydrograph records each having a time length equal to that over which the optimization was to be performed. The use of serial correlations, which required conditional probabilities appearing as matrices, was found to lengthen considerably the computational time with respect to the Monte Carlo procedure. The latter was favored because it developed a larger amount of risk information, and because of its ability to determine more convenient versions of the optimum policy parameters, and to accommodate serially correlated hydrographs.

The Monte Carlo method was also applied to simulate convective diffusions from point sources in both two and three dimensional flow situations [16-18]. The technique was shown to be simple and versatile in studying situations where other techniques—numerical, analytical, or experimental—would have been more cumbersome or have presented substantial difficulties. It was further shown that the effectiveness of the computer program was very sensitive to programming details; small changes in the programs could lead to considerable changes in execution time. In general, the random walk approach was found to use more computer time than a conventional numerical simulation for a comparable situation.

To date, the application of stochastic techniques to hydraulics has generated a substantial body of literature, as exemplified by the Proceedings of a Symposium on Stochastic Hydraulics held at the University of Pittsburgh in 1971 [19].

DYNAMIC PROGRAMMING FOR MULTIPLE STRUCTURES

As the systems that can be designed grow larger and more complex, optimum planning and operation become increasingly important, because even small improvements can result in substantial cost reductions. Dynamic programming, conducted on a large computer, is useful for dealing with system nonlinearities and performance criteria. It can handle extremely general system equations and performance criteria, multiple constraints, and stochastic variations to yield an optimum solution in a feedback control form. The major difficulty in using this method is the computational require-assoicated with a standard computational algorithm, a problem that can be overcome by sophisticated computational procedures.

A review of the state of the art and the implications of dynamic programming applied to complex water resource systems was given by Larson and Keckler [1] in 1969. The authors describe an example of optimization of a four reservoir system used for power generation, irrigation, flood control, and recreation. A policy was established for optimization of the four reservoirs, requiring approximately 30 seconds of computer time on a Burroughs B-5500 for convergence. It was felt that with the computers available in 1969, the optimization could have been extended to a 20 reservoir system.

Deterministic one—dimensional [20] and two—dimensional [21] dynamic programming has been used to determine alternate policies for river basin water quality management [22], [23]. To apply dynamic programming, a river basin such as the one shown in fig. 5-1 can be visualized in the form shown in fig. 5-2. At each stage, decisions or treatment levels are the inputs (D), while the outputs (C) are the local costs for waste treatment.

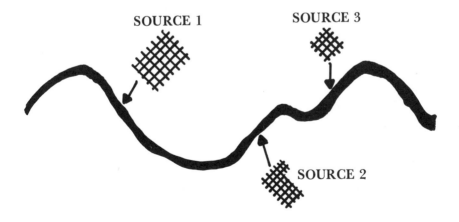

Fig. 5-1. Three sources of waste in a river basin.

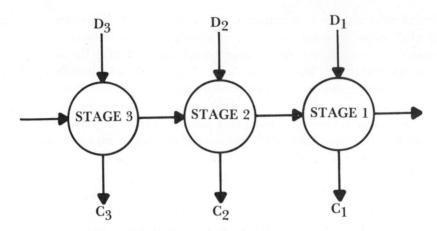

Fig. 5-2. A discrete sequential representation of the river basin in fig. 5-1.

HYBRID SYSTEM—FLOOD STUDIES

A successful example of departure from complex mathematical simulations performed exclusively on digital computers is given by Otoba, Shibatani and Kuwata [24]. By using both digital and analog processes, a combination of precision, flexibility and greater simplicity was achieved, that neither the digital nor the analog computer alone could have made possible. The hybrid system, which used an analog computer in its main assembly, was a specialty machine of large scale not duplicated in other countries. It was applied to the analysis and prediction of floods on the River Kitakami in Japan and yielded water levels and discharges at every instant in the mainstream and branches of the river according to the volume of rainfall, inserted as data on a punched paper tape. Discharge from a dam was simulated by a time program of the function generator, which combined the generator with an integrator. If the rainfall function generator had been composed of analog elements exclusively, it would have presented problems of precision and cost. The hybrid system permitted the use, as an alternative, of one punched tape recording the effective rainfall function; the input data could thus be rapidly read into the digital computer by a phototape reader. The computer's typewriter and phototape reader then become the generator of the rainfall function.

DIGITAL WATERSHED SIMULATION

A milestone in the use of the computer to simulate and thus predict river flow from rainfall was presented by a program developed at Stanford

University. The Mark IV version [25], completed in 1966, was the result of six years of digital hydrologic simulation. Subsequently, the commercial applications of the program—and its further evolution—have been carried out by a private firm, Hydrocomp, set up by the originators of the program [26]. The Mark IV program, which used an IBM 360/67, had the capability of simulating with considerable effectiveness the hydrological behavior of complex river systems. With current information on rainfall and snow runoff, the effects of a flood wave could be calculated at any point downstream.

Basically the simulation model was designed to accept input from any number of recording gages, and to produce flow at a series of points in the stream channel downstream. Streamflow could be calculated at several locations ("flow points") in the stream channel, the area above each location being divided into segments selected from topographical considerations (one or more segments for each recording rain gage). The program allowed for the use of a limitless number of segments. The general model included a data section, and involved reading data cards and storing the data on magnetic tape for use in the simulation. The input to the simulation consisted esentially of options for controlling the program and of fixed parameters determined by watershed characteristics, such as mean rainfall or watershed area. Fig. 5-3 gives the input sequence. The output provided a description of the streamflow conditions at a series of points in the stream channel system, and a number of optional data related to the basic output. The entire simulation model consisted of approximately 1300 statements. The significance of the model was that it could make available to the designer, within a few minutes, information on historically recorded flows and simulated streamflows with a statical estimate of simulation accuracy, and that it offered the opportunity to search out and evaluate all the hydrometeorological records existing in a region.

THERMAL POLLUTION SIMULATION

Simulation of thermal pollution can severely tax the capability of a computer, because the thermal effluent may take a long time before completely mixing with the stream.

The examples in this field are numerous. Characteristically, numerical difference techniques are used to solve a mathematical model of the thermal convective-diffusion process. Thus, Vasiliev, Kvon, and Chernyshova [27] have analyzed thermally stratified flow in streams and reservirs, with warm water flow at one end. Ahlert, Biguria and Tarbell [28] have simulated the

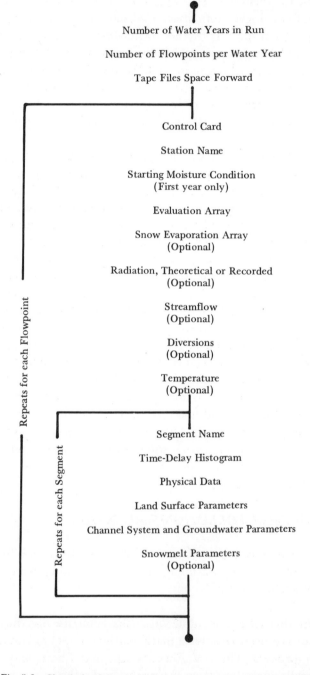

Fig. 5-3. Simulation input sequence for the Stanford Watershed Model IV [25].

dispersion of heat discharged into a steady prismatic flow. A transport model was formulated to describe thermal dispersion and a mesh was used to record the dispersion data. The problem of optimizing the computations became a major one, requiring lengthy (four to six hours) computer runs on an IBM 7090. With a change to the more rapid IBM 360/67 and optimized values of mesh increments, convergence errors were minimized and solutions were obtained in about 10 minutes when using double precision.

LAKE MODELING

A recent study of the state of the art of mathematical modeling for lakes, performed by Hydroscience, Inc. (see Chapter I) for the Great Lakes Basin Commission, showed that the programs necessary to resolve the Great Lakes problems could be established in principle [29]. However, the state of the art is hampered by several problems:

- Incomplete and inconsistant data base
- Insufficient knowledge of basic water circulation and hydrodynamic characteristics
- Inadequate knowledge of interactions among the chemical, physical, and biological aspects of the lakes
- Possibly insufficient computer capabilities for furnishing the quantitative data required for planning purposes.

The impact of the computer in lake modeling as in other kinds of modeling is most evident in two major areas; 1) data handling requirements and 2) processing requirements for analysis. In general, the data required for water resource management and planning models can be categoriezed as:

- Data describing system geometry and geomorphology
- Data describing natural phenomena which input energy or matter into the system
- Data describing inputs from human and cultural activities
- Historical records of the state of the environment.

Ultimately, the models developed must be verified by comparing their output to historical records over a wide range of conditions; for large models, the manipulation of these large quantities of data becomes impossible without the computer. The number of parameters to be handled, the size of the computational increments, and similar factors must then be assessed to determine the computational feasibility of the model. The availability and sophistication of component models or programs (e.g., thermo-dynamic models, ecological models) also plays a major role; these models must be integrated into an overall model.

A common measure for assessing the complexity of integrated models is the "compartment"—a single variable at a single three-dimensional grid point—for example, the concentration of a substance, the magnitude of a velocity, or the number of microorganisms. The computational times for a variety of atmospheric and hydrospheric simulations are shown in fig. 5-4. The greater efficiency of larger computers in handling these tasks is evident. The computational time for simular third generation computers, when estimated over a variety of compartment types, is approximately proportional to the number of compartments in the model. This is shown by the upper solid line in fig. 5-5; the lower solid line in the same figure shows corresponding computation times with the recently developed pipeline or parallel processor machines (see Chapter II). An execution time of 3-10 hours per run seems to be the feasible limit (assuming a nominal $32,000/month or $200/hr for computer time, this amounts to $2000 per run) and corresponds to 70,000 or less compartments.

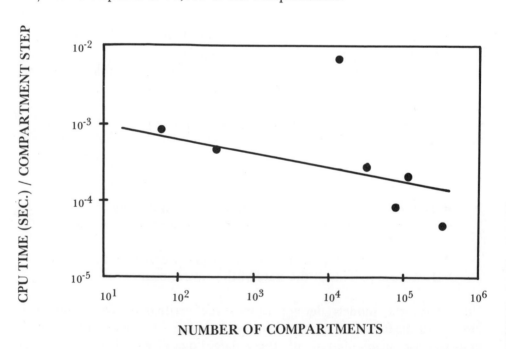

Fig. 5-4   Compartment calculation times (adapted from [29]).

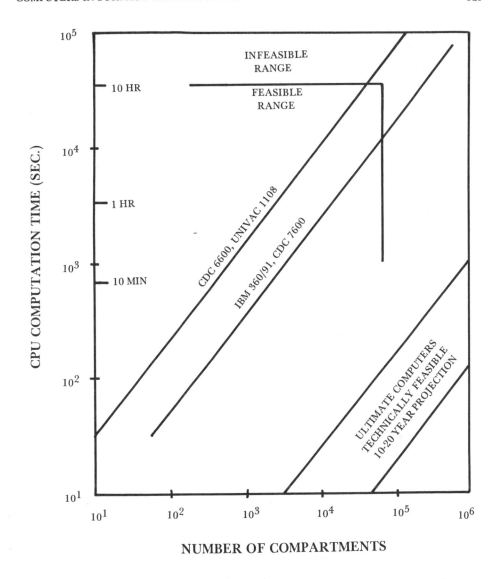

Fig. 5-5.   CPU time to compute a one year simulation, $\triangle t = .1$ day (adapted from [10]).

Another measure of complexity is given by the number of dependent variables versus computation time (fig. 5-6). Assuming a one year simulation and a five layer model with two horizontal spacings ($\triangle X = 5$ km, $\triangle X = 20$ km), and again assuming a feasible limit of 10 hours per run, the figure indicates that about 16 to 150 variables are feasible for a 20 km spacing, while only about 5 to 10 are feasible for a 5 km spacing.

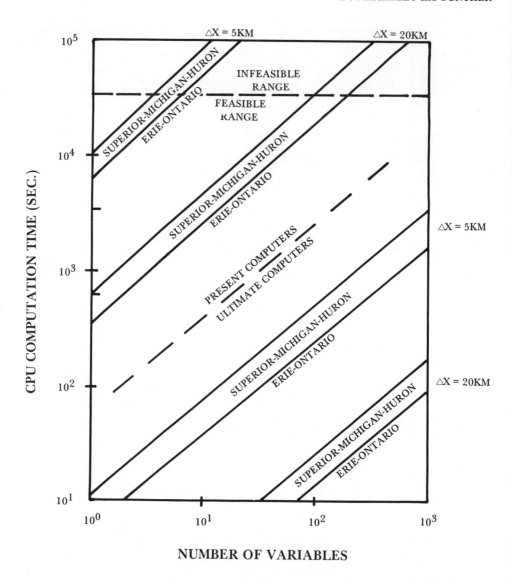

Fig. 5-6.   CPU time to compute one year simulation at five levels in depth for various
horizontal spacing, $\triangle X$ = 5KM, 20KM, $\triangle t$ = 0.1 day (adapted from [29]).

OPTIMAL CONTROL THEORY—AERATION

In 1970, Davidson and Bradshaw described a steady state optimal design
of artificially-induced aeration in polluted streams, using Pontryagin's

Minimum Principle [30]. The authors compared analog and digital computer solutions for the optimization problem by analyzing three different methods of solution. One method used the Riccati-Kalman technique to solve linear quadratic optimal control problems; computations were carried out on an IBM 7090/94 system using an Automatic Synthesis Program (ASP). Another method used an analog computer (also see [31]) solution based upon the use of a Hamiltonian function; computations were carried out on a EAI-8800 computer, which contained a five-place digital voltmeter for greater accuracy in setting potentiometers and reading voltages. The system was stabilized through the use of a feedback limiter, and although the necessary integration was inherently unstable, the method was considered sufficient for the needs of the practitioner. To combine the advantages of the accuracy of the Riccati-Kalman method with the simplicity of the analog computer method, the authors devised a third method, a LaPlace transform technique carried out on a medium sized digital computer. By utilizing the difference equations previously used on the analog computer and by redefining the variables in the equations, a form was generated which lent itself to a LaPlace transformation; the result was then programmed on an EAI-8400 digital computer, the optimal solution being obtained by making iterations on this transformed equation.

TOTAL WATER RESOURCE MANAGEMENT—SIMULATION

A major example of a systems simulation for the management of a total water resource [32], [33] is given by a joint study performed by the Texas Water Development Board and Water Resources Engineers, Inc. The study has been conceived as a first step toward developing a computer-oriented methodology for the planning, design, long range operation, and management of a large multi-basin water resource. The Texas water system is a complex network of service reservoirs, canals, and pumping stations scheduled to handle almost ten million acre-feet of water annually, over a distance of over 700 miles, and through a difference in elevation of over 3500 feet [34]. Total expected cost of the system is in excess of ten billion dollars.

The study uses eight inter-related computer programs—four data management programs and four simulation-optimization ones—coupled with procedures for program use. The data management programs provide the user with a convenient means for organizing the data required by the simulation-optimization programs. The simulation-optimization programs, in turn, define such parameters as when to construct reservoirs and transfer links, reservoir capacity, operating policies, etc., so that construction, operation, and maintenance costs can be minimized.

The planning, carried out in four phases, involved a network of eighteen reservoirs, thirty canals, and twelve river reaches, spanning approximately five hundred miles. The first phase (Phase I) dealt with the sizing of the system elements and with the operating rules of the reservoirs. Phase II was an initial screening of the optimum combination of sizes, schedules, and operating rules. Phase III was a secondary screening and Phase IV the final screening, yielding the recommended water resource plan, the final schedule of operation, and the final sizes of the components of the plan.

At the core of the four planning phases are six computer programs:

- ALLOCATION PROGRAM
- VOLSTG
- EXPLOR

- MSP
- SIM I
- SIM II

VOLSTG, EXPLOR, SIM I, and SIM II operate as subroutines in a comprehensive program, the STAGE DEVELOPMENT PROGRAM. The ALLOCATION PROGRAM, which occurs in Phase I as well as in Phase IV, receives as inputs the average or actual inputs of the system and the maximum or actual demands, and produces optimum operating rules and sizes and optimum construction schedules. The VOLSTG program receives as inputs reservoir sizes and sequences of actual inputs and actual demands, and produces selected schedules using an "out-of-kilter" algorithm; it is essentially a deterministic procedure. The EXPLOR provides a means for randomly selecting the dates when reservoirs and canals might be added to the system. The dates for placing an element of the system in service are considered to be the decision variables, equal in number to the total of the reservoirs or canals, as yet unscheduled.

The MSP program applies the method of successive perturbations to find a low point on the response surface that corresponds to the least costly sequence for placing reservoirs and canals in service. A single application of the MSP system cannot guarantee an absolute minimum, and the MSP system is thus applied from several low starting points to improve the probability of finding the least costly alternative. The input to MSP consists of low cost sequences obtained from the VOLSTG or the EXPLOR programs.

SIM I and SIM II are two simulation programs. The former describes the hydraulic behavior of the system and estimates the cost of storage, conveyance, and purchase of water. The system is characterized as a simplified tree-shaped configuration of nodes (reservoir or non-storage junctions) and connecting links (canals or river reaches); the program solves a simultaneous set of equations derived from mass balances about the nodes. SIM II utilizes an "out-of-kilter" algorithm to find the least costly pattern of operation for the system; a wide range of system considerations and the consequences of constraints in size or operation can be explored.

The increasing effectiveness of the sequential application of these programs is a significant example of optimization by stages. Initial estimates of the system costs over the 36-year planning period, obtained by applying SIM I in the initial screening phase (Phase II), ranged upward from 6.31 billion dollars. By use of the MSP program, the proposed implementation schedule was modified and the cost was reduced to 6.07 billion. In the subsequent phase (Phase III) a secondary screening was applied to the system by employing SIM II with no flow limits on canals. The resultant cost was 7.15 billion, which was further reduced to 5.93 billion after adjusting canal sizes. In the final screening phase (Phase IV), using the allocation program, a slight rescheduling of two system elements removed a deficit condition experienced earlier, and the program could then be applied successfully to a projected 23-year sequence. With sufficient data to secure reliable estimates of costs for the entire 36-year period, the alternative plan was estimated at a total of 4.6 billion dollars (the primary reason for the reduced cost was smaller canal sizes).

Computationally, computer capacity and speed determine the limits to the size of the network that can be considered. It was estimated that with the existing computer codes used by the program and a computer core storage of 60,000 words, it would be possible to analyze a network of up to 30 reservoirs and/or canal junctions, 35 canal links, and 600 time increments (months). However, the program is not practical for a very small system such as a single reservoir.

The report on the Texas study stresses the fact that while the technique cannot guarantee selection of a minimum cost solution, it can enhance the likelihood of making greatly improved decisions. This approach cannot be utilized without further study and the adaptation of procedures for power generation, recreation, flood control, water quality management, and conservation. The report recognizes the desirability of refining the procedure by 1) organized sensitivity testing, 2) training planners in the use of the approaches and techniques developed in the study, and 3) applying the approach to other complex water resource systems.

A progress report on the implementation of the system suggests that the analysis of risk and uncertainty be incorporated in the planning, because of the stochastically varying nature of streamflows, water losses, and water demand data [34]. The use of stochastically generated data permits the simulation and optimization of designs incorporating systems of reservoirs and canals of greater complexity and size.

The necessity of computer analysis in the successful design of waterway systems, especially designs including navigational and hydro-electric power generation facilities, cannot be overstressed. The effect of a lack of analysis is exemplified by the inadequacy of the Apalochicola River system to maintain both power and navigational requirements. The system was designed without utilizing computer analysis, primarily for power generation, disregarding navigation requirements. It was thought that navigation requirements could be met by flow augmentation. Later studies showed that the necessary flow augmentation, ". . . would violate the annual distribution of energy and jeopardize (reservoir) capacity requirements specified. . ."[35].

PROCESS CONTROL

The considerations in the previous sections underscore the powerful influence that computerized process control has come to exert on water resources technology, as on other areas of technology. Computers have rapidly become indispensable in controlling water resource systems, processes, and facilities such as distribution networks, flood control systems, reservoirs, and water quality operations, including scheduled operation of thermo-electric plants and scheduled release of pollutants. Since the ability to control a system generally implies an improved operation of the system, process control in water resources has lead to process optimization.

CONTROL AND MONITORING—RIVERS

The monitoring and operation of large river systems is a particular case of process control. Generally, for such systems, process control does not need to be on-line, and acquires operational characteristics quite distinct from those of other water resource process control systems. These characteristics are exemplified by the activities of the Ohio River Division (ORD) of the U.S. Corps of Engineers. The Ohio Basin contains 96 major lakes and reservoirs. Their regulation is the primary responsibility of the Division; regulation of the navigation on the Ohio River is the Division's second major responsibility. To carry out these activities, ORD has developed a major digital computer programming effort [36]. Main goals of the program include minimization of flood damage by effective use of existing reservoirs, optimum use of storage areas through seasonal regulation of multi-purpose pools, and continuous monitoring to ensure the best regulation by the newest procedures. The computer used is a General Electric 425 digital computer (typical of most division offices), installed in 1970, having initially a capacity of 32,000 words of core, subsequently increased to 64,000 words. The system has multi-programming capability and 9 storage units, each with a capacity of 15 million characters.

Supplementing the computer center at ORD are 4 district stations, each containing a General Electric 225 digital computer (typical of district offices) with 8,000 word storage.

Major programs in use at ORD include: a program for the heat budget analysis of reservoirs, a flood routing program based on the Muskingum method, and three programs for the regulation of reservoirs and navigation dams. The first of these three programs involves a principal daily routing program, which routes flow from Dashields, Pennsylvania to Metropolis, Illinois, through eleven reaches. The second program determines peak flow amounts that can safely be released while keeping movable dams up, so as not to impede navigation. The third program performs a reservoir storage analysis for all tributaries in the Ohio Basin.

The four ORD districts use a total of over 60 programs and subroutines. Some of the important needs listed by ORD in order to better monitor and control the river show the link between process control and hydraulic and hydrologic analysis. They include improved unit hydrographs, studies of cover and geology of hydrologic units for improved estimations of differences in storm runoff, improved ratings for gages set at reservoirs and dams, increased automation at many levels of operation, coordination of activities at the state and federal level as well as with other Corps offices, and increased computer core storage area over and above what the GE 425 computer could supply.

THE CALIFORNIA AQUEDUCT

The California Aqueduct offers an elaborate example of a process control installation spanning approximately 500 miles [37]. The operational structure of part of the system is shown in fig. 5-7. The system consists of approximately 100 "off the shelf" computers (Hewlett Packard, Honeywell, General Electric, etc.) that control the distribution, pumping, etc. of water in the aqueduct. A Project Operation Control Center (POCC), using a Univac 418, analyzes water and power demands, and schedules the operation of the system. The schedule is transmitted to an Area Control Center (ACC) where an operator analyzes certain monitored data and decides what must be done next. Once the decision is made, the computer is used to determine what actions are required to implement the decision, and appropriate instructions are forwarded to the Remote Sites (RS) for action.

Several points are noteworthy. In most stages of the process, the operator analyzes the requirements and controls the system. The computer basically serves to pool and analyze incoming data and to provide summary information to the operator. When the decisions are made or a strategy is

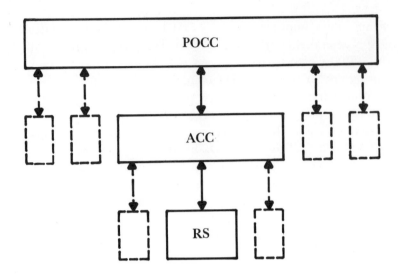

Fig. 5-7.   The structure of the California Aqueduct control system: POCC, Project
Operation Control Center; ACC, Area Control Center; RS, Remote Site.

established, the computer automatically controls the various valves and other physical control devices to accomplish the desired operation. For example, the decision to maintain a certain flow rate may require that the computer control a number of pumps, valves, etc., and constantly pool information on current conditions. The system builds up from the control of a simple valve to the control of major components of the system; at each stage, the computer assumes an increasing number of decision-making tasks.

REFERENCES

[1]   Larson, R. and Keckler, W., Application of Dynamic Programming to the Control of Water Resources Systems, *Automatica, Journal of the International Federation of Automatic Control.* 5, 1969.

[2]   Lawler, E.A. and Druml, F.U., Hydraulic Problem Solution on Electronic Computers, *Journal of the Waterways and Harbors Division,* ASCE, 84, 1958, 1515-1-38.

[3]   Isaacson, E., Stoker, J.J., and Troesch, A., Numerical Solution of Flow Problems in Rivers, *Journal of the Hydraulics Division,* ASCE, 84, 1958, 1810-1-18.

[4]   Rockwood, D.M., Columbia Basin Streamflow Routing By Computer, *Journal of the Waterways and Harbors Division,* ASCE, 84, 1958, 1874-1-15.

[5]   Swain, F.E. and Riesbol, H.S., Electronic Computers Used for Hydrologic Problems, *Journal of the Hydraulics Division,* ASCE, 85, 1959, 21-29.

[6]   Harbeck, G.E. and Isherwood, Jr., W.L., Digital Computers for Water Resources Investigations, *Journal of the Hydraulics Division,* ASCE, 85, 1959, 31-38.

[7]   Grimes, P.R. and Von Gunten, G.H., Electronic Computer Use In Scoping Power Projects, *Journal of the Power Division*, ASCE, 87, 1961, 1-6.

[8]   Catanzaro, E.W., Grady, D.R., and Zaleiko, N.S., Automated Stream Analysis, *Power Engineering*, 72, 1968, 45-48.

[9]   Mirick, R., Computer Programs Used to Collect, Store and Analyze Data Received From the New England Division Automatic Hydrologic Radio Reporting System, *Proceedings*, of a Seminar on Computer Applications in Hydrology, Hydrologic Engineering Center, Davis, California, 1971, 1-9.

[10] Cooper, S., Regulation of Complex Reservoir Systems For Flood Control, *Proceedings*, of a Seminar on Computer Applications in Hydrology, Hydrologic Engineering Center, Davis, California, 1971, 1-14.

[11] Granthan, G.R., Schaake, Jr., J.C., and Pyatt, E.E., Water Quality Simulation Model, *Journal of the Sanitary Engineering Division*, ASCE, 97, 1971, 569-585.

[12] Mills, W.C. and Synder, W.M., Algorithm for Adjusting Stream Stage Records, *Journal of the Irrigation and Drainage Division*, ASCE, 97, 1971, 51-58.

[13] Hall, W.A. and Howell, D.T., The Optimization of Single-Purpose Reservoir Design With the Application of Dynamic Programming to Synthetic Hydrology Samples, *Journal of Hydrology*, 1, 1963, 355-363.

[14] Bellman, R.E., *Dynamic Programming*, Princeton University Press, Princeton, New Jersey, 1957.

[15] Cashwell, E.D. and Everett, C.J., *A Practical Manual on the Monte Carlo Method for Random Walk Problems*, Pergamon Press, London, 1959.

[16] Bugliarello, G. and Jackson III, E.D., Random Walk Study of Convective Diffusion, *Journal of the Engineering Mechanics Division*, ASCE, 90, 1964, 49-77.

[17] Bugliarello, G. and Jackson III, E.D., Random Walk Simulation of Convective Diffusion from Instantaneous Point Sources in a Laminar Field, *Proceedings*, Midwestern Mechanics Conference, 1965, 461-472.

[18] Bugliarello, G. and Jackson III, E.D., Study of Convective Diffusion from Continuous Point Sources by a Random Walk Model, *Proceedings*, 5th U.S. National Congress of Applied Mechanics, ASME, New York, 1966 (Abstract).

[19] Chiu, C.L. (Editor), *Stochastic Hydraulics*, University of Pittsburg, School of Engineering Publication Series, No. 4, 1971.

[20] Dysart, B.C., Alternate Policies for River Basin Water Quality Management, *International Association for Hydraulic Research*, 5, 1971, 335-340.

[21] Dysart, B.C., Water Quality Planning in the Presence of Interacting Pollutants, *Journal Water Pollution Control Federation*, 42, Part 1, 1970, 1515-1529.

[22] Shih, C.S., Dynamic Optimization for Industrial Waste Treatment Design, *Journal Water Pollution Control Federation*, 41, 1969, 1787-1802.

[23] Shih, C.S., System Optimization for River Basin Water Quality Management, *Journal Water Pollution Control Federation*, 42, 1970, 1792-1804.

[24] Otaba, K., Shibatani, K., and Kuwata, H., Food Simulator for the River Kitakami, *Simulation*, 4, 1965, 86-98.

[25] Crawford, N.H. and Linsley, R.K., *Digital Simulation in Hydrology: Standord Watershed Model IV*, Dept. of Civil Engineering, Stanford University, Technical Report No. 39, July 1966.

[26] Crawford, N.H., personal communications, President, Hydrocomp, Inc., Palo Alto, California, 1973.

[27] Vasiliev, O.F., Kvon, V.I., and Chernyshova, R.T. Mathematical Modeling of the Thermal Pollution of a Water Body, *Proceedings*, XVth Congress of International Association for Hydraulic Research, 2, 1973, B17-1-8.

[28] Ahlert, R.C., Biguria, G., and Tarbell, J., Some Finite Difference Solutions for the Dispersion of Thermal Sources in Steady Prismatic Flow, *Water Resources Research*, 6, 1970, 614-621.

[29] Crook, L.T., *Interdisciplinary Modeling of Limnological Aspects of the Great Lakes for Planning Purposes*, Great Lakes Basin Commission, Ann Arbor, Michigan, June 1973, 51 pp.

[30] Davidson, B., and Bradshaw, R.W., A Steady State Optimal Design of Artificial Induced Aeration in Polluted Streams by the Use of Pontryagin's Minimum Principle, *Water Resources Research*, 6, 1970, 333-397.

[31] Davidson, B. and Hunter, J.V., *Process Control Model for Oxygen Regeneration of Polluted Streams*, Water Resources Research Institute, Rutgers—The State University, March 70.

[32] Texas Water Development Board and Water Resources Engineers, Inc., *Systems Simulation for Management of a Total Water Resource*, Completion Report, May 1970.

[33] Texas University, Department of Mechanical Engineering, *Use of New Analytical Methods in Water Resource Development*, Water Pollution Control Series, September, 1970.

[34] Meier, Jr., W.L., Weiss, A.O., Puentes, C.D., Optimum Water Management Under the Texas Water Plan, *International Association for Hydraulic Research*, 5, 1971.

[35] Pierce, H.D., The Need for and Development of a Computer Program for Re-establishing Low Flow Navigation Requirements on the Apalachicola River, *Proceedings*, of a Seminar on Computer Applications in Hydrology, Hydrologic Engineering Center, Davis, California, 1971, p. 7.

[36] Matthews, J.S., Computer Use in Regulating the Ohio River Projects, *Proceedings*, of a Seminar on Computer Applications in Hydrology, Hydrologic Engineering Center, Davis, California, 1971, 1-9.

[37] Cosper, A., personal communications, California Department of Water Resources, Sacramento, California, 1973.

VI. COMPUTERS IN GROUNDWATER SYSTEMS

Groundwater systems like surface water systems, have proved fertile ground for the use of computers. Groundwater technology is concerned with water in the interstices of a confined or unconfined aquifer system. As in other areas of water resource technology, the pertinent problems can be grouped into three main categories:

- Description of the natural physical processes occurring in groundwater flow (both in terms of water quantity and quality)
- Design of man-made devices or processes to modify the characteristics of the natural processes
- Planning and managing groundwater as a resource.

The description of groundwater as a physical process considers flow, heat transfer, and mass transfer aspects, and involves problems which range from finding suitable equations to describe each aspect, to the description of the physical and chemical properties and of the boundary and initial conditions of the groundwater, to the solutions of the equations.

The range of man-made structures and processes affecting groundwater is very broad, and expands as new needs and inventive approaches emerge. Examples are diaphragms, wells, spreading beds, salt water intrusion, earth subsidence phenomenon, and injection of pollutants. The problems involved are basically of two types: a) description of how the physicochemical characteristics of the resource are affected by man-made structures or processes; and b) design of such structures or processes. The first type of problem has the same nature as the problem of resource description, but with different boundary and initial conditions. Problems of the second type are extremely varied, ranging from structural to hydraulic to soil mechanics design.

The problems in managing groundwater as a resource—as a source of water, or as a sink for dispersal of pollutants—usually resolve themselves into the question of how to optimize the resource to achieve a given objective or set of objectives.

In principle, the number and complexity of the variables involved increases as one proceeds from problems of physical description to problems of design or interaction, to problems of planning and management (because planning and management encompass design and interaction, which in turn encompass physical description). In practice, however, it is often possible not to compound the complexity—to do for instance planning on the basis of very simple models of the physical process. In any case, as complexity increases, the use of the computer becomes essential to handle the large number of variables and decision points.

Planning, management, physical design, and physical description were of course possible even before the advent of the computer, but could be carried out only through very simplified hypotheses. Even today, in spite of advances in optimization theory and process control, the ability to deal with completely realistic situations in groundwater planning or to exert detailed management control is far from being attained. The power of contemporary computers and the state of the art of the necessary methodologies remain insufficient. Nor are there fully satisfactory and realistic solutions to the problems of the physical description of the groundwater process. Computer methods have made it possible to go far beyond simple geometries and steady flows, but the complete description of the quality and quantity aspects of groundwater flow, under complex boundary and initial conditions, and for complex physicochemical soil characteristics, are still in the future. In general, analytic procedures are effective when aquifer conditions are uniform and boundary geometries are regular. When these conditions do not exist, an analog computer can provide a solution by modeling techniques. In very complex situations, the answer lies in numerical methods and the digital computer becomes indispensable.

In this chapter, we give a brief historical overview of the use of the computer in groundwater problems, followed by a few examples in the area of analysis and design. We shall not dwell on data collection and process control for groundwater systems, because the pertinent considerations are essentially the same as those for other water resource systems discussed elsewhere in this book. In particular, since current groundwater data collection systems remain less automated and less sophisticated than those of the surface water and water utilization segments, and the data management employed does not differ from that mentioned in Chapter IV, we will not re-examine those areas. Furthermore, since groundwater flow is not readily adaptable to computer-oriented process control, few examples exist of elaborate control systems.

HISTORICAL NOTES

Physical groundwater problems differ from those of surface water in the sense that they lend themselves more readily and effectively to the application of analog computers, which were historically the first to be used in groundwater flow, and came to play a relatively greater role than in other fields of water resource technology. Initial developments were slow, but by the early 60's the analog computer could already solve problems of greater complexity than were practical with analytic methods. Analog models were found to be reusable, easily assembled, and to closely resemble the actual hydrologic system.

In the early 60's, comparisons with digital computers showed analog computers to be generally less expensive and, in many cases, to provide faster computation. Additionally, no instructions were required concerning the mathematical methods involved in the solution of a problem. Studies performed on analog computers were considered to be limited only by the magnitude and cost of the effort required to collect sufficient data to fully describe the aquifers.

The state of the art at the beginning of the 60's is exemplified by a paper by Skibitzke [1], which discusses the application of an analog computer to the development of groundwater supplies for communities. Such development projects require the determination of the water level changes in and around the groundwater storage area. Where thin water table aquifers produce only small changes in the water level, an accurate and well-defined analysis of the area under development can usually only be accomplished with the aid of a computer. To describe the hydraulic characteristics of an aquifer, an electrical element was used as an analog to an element of the aquifer, as shown in fig. 6-1 [1]. The electrical element consisted of a junction, with six resistors (A-F) flowing into it and a capacitor (G) to ground. The resistors were made proportional to the hydraulic resistance in directions parallel to the three coordinate axes (X, Y, Z), and the capacitor made proportional to the storage coefficient.

A model consisting of many of these junctions allowed the hydrologic characteristics of the aquifer to be mapped in three dimensions. Days could be made proportional to a few microseconds on an oscillograph connected to the analog model at any point where the changes in water level with respect to time were to be determined. Many situations could be simulated—such as tidal fluctuations, well discharge, and recharge from rainfall—by the adjustment of an electrical current flow (analogous to the hydraulic flow) into and out of the model, and by recording the potential at each desired point.

By 1961, it became evident that further computer developments were hampered by the lack of additional descriptive information concerning aquifers and by limitations in geologic and engineering methodology. Computer techniques necessary to describe most hydrologic systems seemed

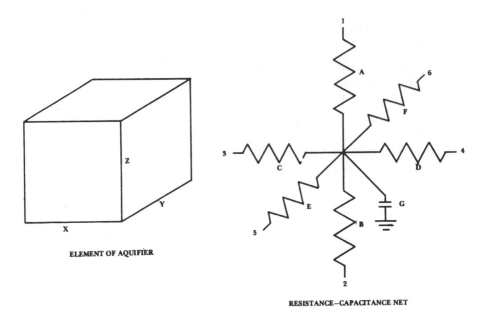

Fig. 6-1.   A diagram showing the relationship between hydraulic and electronic elements [1].

to be theoretically feasible, but cost was, in most cases, a major obstacle. Thus, reduction of the cost of model construction and simplification of the electronic linkages needed for the description of boundary conditions were considered as areas of major research needs. Very little work had been done by 1961 on free surfaces, because of their complex nature.

As another example of the state of the art in the early 60's, Walton and Prickett [2] discuss the construction and operation of analog computers for forecasting conditions in non-homogeneous aquifers having irregular shapes and boundaries, and with various head and discharge controls.

The specific analog computer described by Walter and Prickett consisted of an analog model and an excitation-response apparatus. The analog model was again an array of resistors and capacitors (as many as 416 resistors and 225 capacitors) representing respectively the hydraulic conductivitiy and the storage of water in an aquifer. The excitation-response apparatus consisted of a wave-form generator, a pulse generator, and an oscillograph; the generators were used to excite the model, and the oscillograph displayed voltage changes with respect to time in response to the excitation. The results were used to construct a map which displayed water level changes at all points in the aquifer. Useful evaluations were obtained with the analog computer even when the analyses were based on incomplete data and idealized mathematical models. The accuracy of an analog solution was generally dependent on the quality of the resistors and capacitors of the model and on the signal to noise ratio. Models simulating three aquifer situations that occurred in Illinois showed close agreement between analog computer and analytic solutions; differences between the two solutions were not judged significant, considering the accuracy and adequacy of the geologic and hydrologic data.

By the end of the decade, experiences such as the ones we have described led to the conclusion that the analog computer was an effective tool for correlating large amounts of data pertaining to both surface and groundwater flows and their interactions. Visual displays connected to the analog computer were found to be very useful when correlating data such as those obtained in surface and groundwater flow problems. Ease of programming and immediate output greatly simplified the task of obtaining solutions of problems which are best solved by applying successive trial processes. By proper selections of resistance and capacitance, the analog operation could be slowed and read out directly on a writing oscillograph.

Recently, however, the picture has begun to change. Rapid advances in numerical methods, increased ability in programming, and faster computing speeds have made the digital computer a very useful computational aid in the analysis of various aspects of a groundwater basin. The digital computer is versatile and requires no major equipment changes to analyze drastically different situations. This suggests, in many cases, a combined use of analog and digital computers, in which the analog is used for a basic preliminary analysis and the digital is used after initial data have been obtained and more detailed analyses are desired. The natural outgrowth of such an approach is the use of hybrid computers, which may well offer the best approach for providing a low cost, accurate, and rapid solution of a groundwater basin problem.

ANALYSIS AND DESIGN

THE RELAXATION METHOD

One of the cardinal elements in the growing popularity of the digital computer in groundwater flow studies has been the development of effective numerical analysis techniques. One of these is the relaxation method, which is essentially a reiteration or "trial and adjustment" procedure [3]. Enger [4], in a review of the method applied to groundwater flow problems, points out that the most significant advantage of the method is the simple and direct treatment of problems. The answers are, of course, approximate, but satisfactory results can be obtained by reducing errors to designated minimums. Enger presents an application of the method to the study of the dynamics of a fresh water-salt water interface in a deep permeable aquifer containing salt water, overlain by a less permeable material, and subject to a surcharge due to irrigation with fresh water. A finite difference equation approximating a second order LaPlace differential equation was used to attack the problem. The two-dimensional model surface was divided into squares, the size of which determined the accuracy of the results, and additional divisions could be selectively placed among areas of a larger division to increase accuracy. The relaxation procedure could easily determine answers to problems concerning density differences, additional loading, multiple soil layers, sloping soil layers, and could also be applied to three-dimensional problems.

In a second example, Finnemore and Perry [5] investigated the problem of seepage flow through a homogeneous earth dam, again using the relaxation method. Assuming that the flow was plane, steady, and governed by Darcy's law, the authors developed a FORTRAN program for the IBM 7090, which required 50-70 seconds for solution. Not only were the results in close (0.5%) agreement with the theoretical formula, but also variations in permeability or other similar effects, which are difficult to handle by classical methods, could be readily incorporated into the computational scheme.

THE FINITE DIFFERENCE METHOD

As a result of the development of high speed digital computers, the finite difference method—essentially the process of replacing derivatives at a point by the ratios of the changes in variables over a finite interval [3]—has been applied to numerous problems in subsurface hydrology. For example, Pinder and Bredehoeft [6] used the implicit finite difference method to analyze unsteady-state flow in a confined aquifer (Musquodoboit Harbour, Nova Scotia). The model, developed on an IBM 360/50/75 (64K), was designed to handle:

- Nonhomogeneous anisotropic porous mediums
- Irregular boundry conditions
- Vertical leakage to the aquifer.

Model verification was accomplished, in part, by constructing an electric analog (similar to that in fig. 6-1) and comparing the results of pumping for selected periods of time.

This numerical method has been applied to a broad range of groundwater problems, some of which include: partially saturated seepage from canals

[7], flow over and through rock-fill banks [8], seepage through dams [9], seepage from ditches [10], flow through heterogeneous media [11], and regional groundwater flow [12]. In the last reference Freeze and Wither-spoon [12] analyzed regional groundwater flow using a three-dimensional, homogeneous, anisotropic basin model. The solution was obtained by programming (FORTRAN IV) an IBM 7094 with 32,000 word storage, which limited the solution to 7500 nodes (25 X 25 X 12). The authors noted that 7500 nodes was obviously not sufficient to represent complicated topographies or complex configurations, but that access to a larger machine would overcome this problem.

Several other advantages of the finite difference method were stated by Remson et. al. [13]: "... a great advantage of the finite-difference digital computer approach is that it is compatible with machine-oriented methods of data storage and retrieval... Machine oriented storage will eventually be used for most types of groundwater data. It is likely that groundwater investigators will have libraries of programs capable of achieving certain types of solutions. It will be necessary only to take the data deck or tape for a given aquifer and the suitable program to a nearby computer to achieve a solution."

THE FINITE ELEMENT METHOD

Unlike the finite difference and other numerical techniques that obtain solutions by working directly with the governing equations, the finite element method, a recent "outgrowth of the high speed computer era" [14], obtains approximate solutions by applying an alternate formulation determined by variational calculus [3]. An application of the method (for a general description of the method see [15]) by France et. al. [16] to the study of free surface, i.e., semi-confined, flow situations (flow through dams, between drains, and toward wells) showed the method to be versatile and general enough to solve many practical seepage problems. These included time-varying cases, which were attacked by using a string of steady state solutions separated by small increments of time. The use of isoparametric elements made it possible to readily analyze seepage through inhomogeneous and anisotropic regions.

The method has been applied to steady state groundwater flow problems [17], [18], transient groundwater flow problems [19], and one-dimensional diffusion-convection problems [14]. As pointed out by Guymon [14], the method not only handles a variety of boundry conditions more easily than the finite difference method, but requires less execution time and storage capacity, thus reducing the cost of solution. However, much further work is required at this moment to bring the finite element method to bear on free surface problems in general.

BASIN STUDIES

The employ of the computer as an essential tool for modeling extensive groundwater basins is exemplified by a model by Williams [20], aimed at providing an accurate time-dependent indication of groundwater levels. The model divides a particular basin area into small sub-areas that are rectangular, square, or of some other polygonal shape; in this fashion, regular shapes can be used to coincide with irregular geologic boundaries. Data levels are assigned to each side and to the interior of the polygons, and the equations governing the flow into or out of a sub-area are based on Darcy's law. The analysis begins from some average water level at the center of a polygon; the computer then calculates inflow, outflow, and storage changes for each sub-area, and calculates a new level at the interior point of the polygon. After some time, Δt, the new levels are in turn used to calculate new inflow, outflow, and storage changes that result in a new level for the interior of each polygon. This process is repeated for some given time period. Normally if hydraulic data were entered on a yearly basis, ten iterations per year would be sufficient to produce the desired accuracy. Data generated from pumping tests can be used to control the design of wells and pumps, the space between wells, and the safe amount of water that can be withdrawn from or added to a particular aquifer storage area in a given time. In the management of a groundwater basin, similar data can be used to determine the future behavior of the reservoir under given conditions.

GROUNDWATER FLOW—HYBRID APPLICATIONS

When dealing with the non-linear partial differential equations of unsteady groundwater flow, which generally have two or more independent variables, the exclusive use of analog methods is undesirable, because analog computers have only one independent variable (time). For example, in the method of discrete space-continuous time (DSCT) introduced by Karplus [21], [22], in which the space variable is discretized and the time variable is left continuous, reasonable analog solutions are obtained rapidly only for non-linear and time-invariant fields. For such fields, a large number of adjustments are needed to the circuit elements, at times without guarantee of solution.

Ditigal computer techniques, on the other hand, are handicapped by the long, costly computer runs necessary to obtain reasonable accuracies. In the solution of transient field problems, all independent and dependent variables in the space and time domain must be discretized. In practice, if the space domain has been sectioned into M finite difference grid points, an M by M matrix must be inverted for each time step to solve the system of finite difference equations. Further iteration at each time step or inversion of the M by M matrix becomes necessary because of the non-linear parameters, until the specified convergence condition is satisfied. This matrix inversion is very costly, absorbing much time and requiring a large storage area.

A discrete space-discrete time (DSDT) hybrid computer method used by Vemuri and Dracup [23] combines the accuracy, memory, decision-making capability, and "programability" of the digital computer with the speed and flexibility of the analog computer. The basic problem is programmed for solution on a digital computer, but it allows loops dealing with matrix inversions to be substituted with corresponding analog resistance networks. These networks act as subroutines in a digital computer loop, performing what would have been very time-consuming digital operations. The iterative process can be automated by connecting the analog resistance network in a closed loop with the digital computer.

The schematic of the discrete space-discrete time (DSDT) computer is shown in fig. 6-2. The analog voltages are sampled at the nodes of the analog resistance network by a multiplexer, converted, and transmitted to the digital computer. Data from the digital computer can be converted through a digital-to-analog converter and applied to the input nodes of the analog resistance network through a distributor. The solution of the partial differential equations in a groundwater flow problem is obtained through two computational phases on the DSDT computer. The first is the identification phase, and demonstrates the versatility of the hybrid computer. Paramaters in the different equations can be determined through the analog resistance network by adjusting the resistors (representing the parameters) until computed water levels match the known historical water level records. This can be done by trial and error with the aid of a CRT display, or by using a combination of steepest descent and random optimization techniques. The second phase, the computational phase, subjects the mathematical model to the various operating conditions which correspond to pumping, artificial recharge, and expected rainfall. This phase may be accomplished most conveniently by using the iterative network previously established.

Although not a hybrid computer in the true sense of the word (as described in Chapter II), the DSDT hybrid computer was found to be more flexible and faster than either the analog or digital computer used alone. If an analog computer were used to duplicate the efforts in phase 1, it would

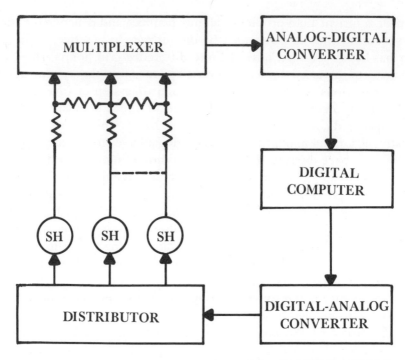

Note: SH— SAMPLE & HOLD

Fig. 6-2. A schematic of a DSDT computer (adapted from [8]).

require costly diode function generators. The alternatives involve either great expense or a reduction in the number of nodes used in the problem. Therefore, the hybrid computer becomes more economical and accurate than the analog computer. On the other hand, in a pure digital computer application, the matrix inversion operation would require extensive storage space and computer running time. Thus, Vemuri and Dracup concluded that a hybrid computer facility utilizing only a small and relatively inexpensive digital computer exhibits the capability of a large digital computer facility. The hybrid computer allows man-machine interaction during the solution process, hence making it possible for the engineer to assist the computer in decisions and to explore alternatives with immediate results. A review of past and current studies on the applicability of DSDT techniques to the solution of hydrology problems and to the simulation of water resource systems is given by Karplus [24].

REFERENCES

[1] Skibitzke, H.E., Electronic Computers as an Aid to the Analysis of Hydrologic Problems, *International Association of Scientific Hydrology*, Publ. 52, 1961.

[2] Walton, W.C. and Prickett, T.A., Hydrogeologic Electric Analog Computers, *Journal*, ASCE, 89, 1963, 67-91.

[3] Remson, I., Hornberger, G.M., and Moltz, F.J., *Numerical Methods in Subsurface Hydrology*, Wiley-Interscience, New York, 1971, 389 pp.

[4] Enger, P.F., Groundwater Flow by Relaxation Methods, ASCE, *Water Resources Engineering Conference*, May 1966.

[5] Finnemore, E.J. and Perry, B., Seepage through an Earth Dam Computed by the Relaxation Technique, *Water Resources Research*, 4, 1968, 1059-1067.

[6] Pinder, G.F. and Bredehoeft, J.D., Application of the Digital Computer for Aquifer Evaluation, *Water Resources Research*, 4, 1968, 1069-1093.

[7] Jeppson, R.W. and Nelson, R.W., Inverse formulation and finite difference solution to partially saturated seepage from canals, *Proceedings*, Soil Science Society of America, 34, 1970, 9-14.

[8] Curtis, R.P. and Lawson, J.D., Flow over and through rock-fill banks, *Journal of the Hydraulics Division*, ASCE, 93, 1967, 1-21.

[9] Jeppson, R.W., Seepage through dams in the complex potential plane, *Journal of the Irrigation and Drainage Division*, ASCE, 94, 1968, 23-29.

[10] Jeppson, R.W., Seepage from ditches—solution by finite differences, *Journal of the Hydraulics Division*, ASCE, 94, 1968, 259-283.

[11] Jeppson, R.W., Free-surface flow through heterogeneous porous media, *Journal of the Hydraulics Division* ASCE, 95, 1969, 363-381.

[12] Freeze, R.A. and Witherspoon, P.A., Theoretical analysis of regional groundwater flow, I: Analytical and Numerical Solutions to the Mathematical Model, *Water Resources Research*, 2, 1966, 641-656.

[13] Remson, I., Appel, C.A., and Webster, R.A., Ground-water models solved by a digital computer, *Journal of the Hydraulics Division*, ASCE, 91, 1965, 133-147.

[14] Guymon, G.L., A Finite Element Solution of the One-Dimensional Diffusion-Convection Equation, *Water Resources Research*, 6, 1970, 204-210.

[15] Zienkiewics, O.C., *The Finite Element Method in Structural and Continuum Mechanics*, McGraw-Hill, London, 1967.

[16] France, P.W., Parekh, C.J., Peters, J.C., and Taylor, C., Numerical Analysis of Free Surface Seepage Problems, *Journal of the Irrigation and Drainage Division*, ASCE, 97, 1971, 165-179.

[17] Zienkiewicz, O., Mayer, P., and Cheung, Y.K., solution of anisotropic seepage by finite elements, *Journal Mechanics Division*, ASCE, 1, 1966, 111-120.

[18] Taylor, R.L., and Brown, C.B., Darcy flow solutions with a free surface, *Journal Hydraulics Division*, ASCE, 2, 1967, 25-33.

[19] Javandel, I. and Witherspoon, P.A., a method of analyzing transient fluid flow in multi-layer aquifers, *Water Resources Research*, 5, 1969, 856-869.

[20] Williams, D.E., Modern Techniques in Groundwater Studies, *Journal American Water Works Association*, 63, 1971, 433-438.

[21] Karplus, W.J., Error Analysis of Hybrid Computer Systems, *Simulation*, 6, 1966, 120-136.

[22] Bekey, G.A. and Karplus, W.J., *Hybrid Computation*, John Wiley and Sons, New York, 1968.

[23] Vemuri, R. and Dracup, J.A., Analysis of Nonlinearities in Groundwater Hydrology: A Hybrid Computer Approach, *Water Resources Research*, 3, 1967, 1047-1058.

[24] Karplus, W.J., and Dracup, J.A., *The Application of the DSDT Hybrid Computer Method to Water Resources Problems*, Water Resources Center, California Univ., Los Angeles, June 1971.

VII. COMPUTERS IN WATER UTILIZATION SYSTEMS

This chapter briefly reviews significant aspects and examples of the use of the computer in water utilization systems—from collection, treatment, and distribution of water supplies to irrigation to waste water collection, treatment and disposal, including the effects of pollution loads on streams and other bodies of water. The computer has become virtually indispensable for analysis, design, and operational control in each of these areas. It is used to select the best sites for water collection and to rapidly design a logically placed distribution system; it plays vital roles in monitoring levels and customer use data, so that water can be routed in proper proportions according to need; it is employed in preparing billing data for utilities, which look hopefully toward the day when water use data can be monitored on an individual basis. In most of these cases the desired information is requested on a minimum cost basis and within specified time constraints, so that construction and maintenance can keep pace with needs.

HISTORICAL NOTES

In January of 1956, the Philadelphia Water Department examined the issue as to whether a McIlroy Network Analyzer could be more effective than hand trial and error calculations for the design of approximately 2900 miles of pipe in its distribution system (pipe ranging in size from 4 to 93 inches) [1]. The McIlroy Analyzer is an example of a dedicated single purpose analog. It consisted basically of a system of electrical resistances which yielded voltage drops analogous to head losses, and currents analogous to flow rates; thus it provided a direct working model of a piping network. Inflow rates could be changed quickly from zero to full system capacity, and trial changes made in minutes. The most significant feature of the analyzer was the ability to rapidly change entire configurations through a patch panel, with minimal disruption.

After reviewing the characteristics of the analyzer, the water department decided to employ it, mainly in analyzing arterial mains. The design tasks for the analyzer included piping, equalization storage, pumping stations, routing, and districting. Two years later, in 1958, the water department used the analyzer (of which 15 were in service at that time throughout the country, but only 3 specifically for water studies) to compute data from high service districts in the City of Philadelphia and to compare the results with digital and general-purpose analog computer solutions [1].

At the same time, digital computers, by using the Hardy-Cross relaxation technique (the most convenient technique developed for hand analyses) could rapidly perform the trial and error iterations required to balance the flow rates initially assumed by the designer. Changes in pipe layout or flow conditions usually required stopping the computer for a few minutes to change several punched cards. Yet, extensive time was consumed in the tedious tabulation and manipulation of data instructions, and afterwards the results had to be summed algebraically before the analysis could be reviewed. Errors were only found after an entire run and often were very difficult to locate. Roughly 50 to 60 punched cards were needed for the basic program instructions; this number increased as the size of the network increased, introducing a greater possibility of error. Furthermore, the digital computer lacked at the time the model visualization feature characteristic of most analog devices such as the McIlroy Analyzer.

As to the general-purpose analog computers, in 1958 the devices required for simulating the nonlinear characteristics of pipelines were unrefined, and analyses had to be restricted mostly to simple systems. Network analyses could be accomplished only through a series of intermediate runs, each with different computations and adjustments. Until the development of a small and simple nonlinear resistance component, general-purpose analogs would remain limited in their capabilities and could not handle complex network problems.

A comparison of the digital computer and the McIlroy Analyzer was also presented in 1958 by Graves and Branscome [2]. The digital computer considered was an IBM 650, classified at the time as a moderate speed, moderate capacity computer. It was employed to solve the Hazen-Williams formula for flow in pipes of a water distribution system through a modification of the Hardy-Cross method. The key advantage found in the digital computer was versatility—it could be used to solve a variety of problems. Although a certain amount of time was necessary to set up the various elements of a program, this effort reduced the time required to write programs to solve various other problems. Additionally, the digital output could be produced directly in hydraulic units. On the other hand, the high purchase or rental costs were a major disadvantage, thus their use was only justified when a large volume of computations was encountered.

In comparing the digital computer to the McIlroy Analyzer, the analyzer was found in turn to have both advantages and dissadvantages. It required only a very simple procedure for altering the potentials at input and output points; the components simulating given elements could be readily removed or altered. On the other hand, the costs of pieces of equipment were high, and there was the need for a specialist to set up the equipment, monitor the results, convert hydraulic units to electrical units, and later convert the electrical output back to hydraulic units. On the balance, Graves and Branscome favored the digital computer—a different conclusion from that of the 1956 analysis by the Philadelphia Water Department. The Philadelphia Department had believed that an analog device provided the best possible utilization of manpower and investment in computational equipment, while Graves and Branscome suggested that the digital computer was more efficient. The first position was basically due to a familiarity with analog devices, acquired through years of use, and to a basic unfamilarity with the digital computer. The second position stemmed from the feeling that although the digital computer was more expensive and required initial familiarization, is still proved to be more efficient. This was so primarily because the time spent in writing a program was considered to offset the time spent in the hydraulic-electrical conversions, required with an analog machine, and could be partially regained by using the program in analyses other than the specific one at hand. This position was ultimately justified by subsequent developments; during the late 50's, a shift occurred from analyzers and analog devices as the major analysis aids, to digital computers.

The first use of a computer—an analog one—to study the effect of waste disposal on a stream occurred in 1958 [3]. It involved the solution of the basic biological oxygen demand (BOD) versus time relationship, and of the Streeter-Phelps oxygen sag equation. The analog computer was thought ideal for this application because the exertion of BOD and the recovery from oxygen depletion behave in the same manner as current through a resistor, and voltage across a capacitor in a circuit. Constants were rapidly determined by directly reading them from the analog, while fitting the electrical curve to an actual curve. The intrinsic simplicity of the approach, and the ability to rapidly produce a number of curves for different conditions, lead to a rapid diffusion of the use of analogs for this purpose. The procedures remained essentially those followed in the 1958 application, except for the use of more sophisticated hardware. By the mid 60's, however, the greater availability and precision of digital computers lead to increasing reliance on digital techniques in this area also.

In 1963, Brock discussed closed loop automatic control of water system operations [4]. In a closed loop or real time "on-line" control system, the computer becomes an indispensable element of the system. For the application and operational method considered by Brock, the digital computer proved to be a better choice than the analog in controlling the closed loop operations. The fact that analog computers required function generators to represent complicated pump inputs made them less desirable, because the generators were expensive, few functions were available, setting up the function generators was quite complex, and translation was required from formulas to electronic parameters.

It was concluded that while the analog computer could be used adequately in the basic analysis of a water network system, both detailed and large-scale analysis with the analog were prohibitive, because of the increasing total cost for additional required equipment, which in general was not commercially available. Digital computers, on the other hand, were able to handle with greater ease the large number of parameters required for such analyses.

The position in the Brock paper gathered strength, particularly because already in the early 60's, digital computers were being designed with systems flexibility in mind so that a particular computer could be sold to various customers and tailored to suit their storage needs and input/output requirements. Another consideration which became important was the personnel needed for the operation of the computer. It was found that the average graduate engineer could operate a sophisticated computer system, once technical people outlined its operation.

By the mid 60's significant advances had also occurred in the application of digital computers to the analysis of distribution systems. Characteristically it become possible to:

- Preset the initial flow pattern
- Balance the system in a reasonable number of iterations
- Compute all gradients and pressures within the system so that manual calculations became unnecessary
- Handle all facilities, such as pumping stations, storage tanks, and in-line boosters
- Handle three-dimensional problems
- Establish internal indexing and parameter designation which allowed input data to be in any order
- Generate error messages for incomplete or inconsistent data
- Achieve complete program control by controlling accuracy limitations, maximum number of iterations, over relaxation factors (to accelerate convergence), and type and amount of output desired.

An example of these features was encountered in the design of the municipal water systems for three communities in Missouri: Florissant

(50,000 inhabitants), Kirkwood (30,000) and Webster Grove (30,000) [5]. The Florissant system, first studied in 1963, was represented by a network of approximately 50 loops and 300 lines. An IBM 7072 was used for the analysis in conjunction with a library program from the University of Washington, which was based on the Hardy-Cross method and the Hazen-Williams flow formula. About 10 minutes of machine time (300 iterations) were required to balance the system within an accuracy of 0.001 MGD (million gallons/day). For every line and every loop, print outs gave the balance flow, in million gallons per day and in gallons per minute, as well as head loss in feet. Much engineering time was consumed in establishing the initial flow pattern and in evaluating the results.

Approximately 100 loops, 300 lines, and 6 loading conditions were used in analyzing the Kirkwood system. Problems arose with pipes running parallel to other pipes but not connecting at the same points (this created in essence a three dimensional effect which required a change in the program). Each analysis used approximately four minutes of machine time (25 iterations) to achieve an accuracy of 0.01 MGD. Later a new program was developed which gave printed outputs in a more useable form, eliminated manual calculations for interpreting the outputs, and delegated to the computer the time-consuming task of determining the initial flow pattern. The program was found to be versatile, with virtually no limitation on the size of the network. In designing system improvements, the exact pipe diameter required could be obtained by proceeding from the smallest diameter, analyzing the system, progressively increasing the pipe size and re-analyzing the system, until all system design conditions were satisfied.

ANALYSIS AND DESIGN

DISTRIBUTION SYSTEMS

The cost of a distribution system (or network) may amount to 50% or more of the entire cost of a water supply system. Thus optimization of the cost-benefit ratio of the system is a major design objective, and the computer has become indispensible to its achievement. Numerous methods have been developed for this purpose. A recent example is the equivalent diameter method, which uses cost functions to provide optimum economical analyses of a pipe network [6]. In this method, all pipe branches in the network are replaced by equal lengths of pipes with an equivalent diameter. By using assumed pressure surfaces throughout the network, the most economical pipe sizes can be determined. To obtain the optimal solution of any particular network, the analysis must be carried out several times for various inlet hydraulic heads and pressure surfaces; the computer is essential for this method to be productive, and general computer programs have been developed, for analyzing different types of networks.

The numerous alternatives possible in the design of a water distribution system makes the application of dynamic programming a powerful tool. Through decomposition techniques, stage-wise optimization becomes possible, converting the problem from a multiple decision single-stage one to a multiple stage single-decision one [7]. Linear programming has also been effectively used in a number of applications both with tree-like and looped networks [e.g., 8,9].

The process of designing a water distribution system can be assisted by the utilization of interactive systems which allow the designer to rapidly explore and heuristically evaluate (using a CRT for example) a large number of system configurations. This approach is particularly powerful when coupled with dynamic programming or other approaches for finding least cost networks [10].

WASTE WATER COLLECTION

The use of computers in the design and operation of waste water collection works is analogous to that in the design and operation of water distribution systems. Basically, the same considerations apply. The computer makes it possible to:

- Estimate design flow by calculating or simulating all flows received from any point and accumulated in the system
- Compute partial flows, to determine minimal or average flows in the sewer lines
- Check input data and elements of the output
- Design sewers to accomodate the design flows
- Produce a detailed listing of costs from unit prices applied to design data
- Develop cost estimates and construction information
- Optimize the collection process.

An early example of comprehensive computer use is the design of an 80 mile sewer system for Nassau County's new district in Long Island. A group of consulting engineers [11] using the IBM 7040 at the Polytechnic Institute of Brooklyn (now the Polytechnic Institute of New York) achieved a more precise design than possible by conventional procedures alone. An economical exploration of alternatives, and redesign, became feasible by continuously monitoring cost estimates.

In three separate analyses, the input data were optimized and designs and cost estimates were produced in 12 minutes; partial flow data for the entire system were obtained in 5 minutes. The analyses were accomplished with 4 basic programs and 53 subroutines. The programs required nearly three years to complete, and were checked against a design made previously by conventional methods. As a result of the success of the approach, the County Public Works Commissioner chose to use it in the design of the sewers for the new district on Long Island's South Shore.

As in the case of water distribution systems, identification of least cost solutions can be achieved by linear programming, dynamic programming, as well as by iterative techniques, although applications of these techniques to date have not been as extensive. A recent example of a discrete dynamic programming application is given by Merritt and Bogan [12].

TREATMENT PLANT DESIGN

Stricter pollution abatement laws have caused an increase in demand for sewage treatment plant designs—a demand that cannot be satisfied within the allocated time by the number of available designers. The problem can be alleviated by resorting to the computer for the performance of those tasks that do not require engineering judgment, such as repetitive design calculations, drafting, and editing specifications [13]. For example, a software system capable of producing a bid package of drawings and specifications has been developed recently by Technicomp Inc., a computer consulting firm. Working with Quirk, Lawler, and Matusky [14], a consulting firm specializing in treatment plant design [15], the task was subdivided into three major components:

- Establishing a data base containing manufacturer's equipment specifications
- Programming the design and analysis process
- Developing software to generate engineering drawings for the resultant design.

Written in FORTRAN IV for an IBM 1130 (8K), the system uses inputs such as sewage flow, pollutant concentration, effluent restrictions and the manufacturer's data base. The inputs are analyzed through routines for structural analysis, process design, site considerations, process flow, hydraulics, and solids balance. The outputs of these routines are dimensions, elevations, reinforcing steel sizes, etc. that serve as inputs to the second phase—the production of specifications and drawings. Since it quickly became evident that a small plotter would not suffice, considerable effort was devoted to generating a compiler capable of producing an output compatible with available software/hardware drafting machine configurations. (Today few drafting languages are capable of handling the diverse problems encountered in treatment plant design.)

Searching for the least cost size of a treatment plant demands the use of optimization techniques, particularly in the case of plants with multiple units of the same type. A number of computer programs have been developed for this purpose [e.g., 16].

Biological Processes in Water Treatment Plants and in Streams

The computer, both analog and digital, has proved to be a particularly useful tool in the analysis of biological processes associated with waste water treatment and dispatch. For instance, analog computers have been shown to be very effective in the analysis of the activated sludge process—a common treatment method for organic wastes. Their application for this purpose was considered seriously for the first time in 1958 by the American Association of Professors of Sanitary Engineering [17]. The activated sludge process is described by a set of simultaneous non-linear differential equations for the bio-oxidation rate. A study by Burkhead and Wood [18], in which various types of feed inputs were applied to different activated sludge systems, has shown that the analog computer can:

- Solve the non-linear differential equations employed in the design of completely mixed activated sludge systems
- Produce solutions both for steady state and transient conditions (the latter present considerable difficulties with other computational approaches; however, the effectiveness of the analog is currently limited by our imperfect knowledge as to the ability of present design expressions to describe transient changes in actual treatment plants)
- Determine operational changes produced by various plant influents
- Make comparisons possible of the response of different systems to varied influences.

Basically, a water resources system represents a giant reactor for the biological cycle occurring in it. The computer makes it possible to consider in its entirety the cycle by studying the balance between the bacteria that oxydize organic matter and free nutrients, and the phytoplankton that reduces minerals and resynthetizes organic materials for life support. The eutrophication process—the excessive growth of algae and the exhaustion of dissolved oxygen—is at a minimum when balance is achieved between these two elements. The increases and decreases of zooplankton, fish, detritus, BOD nutrients and dissolved oxygen can be described by a set of simultaneous differential equations.

In an example of computer application, a model of a hypothetical stream ten feet deep and fifty feet wide was segmented lengthwise into 1500-ft. elements [19]. The set of simultaneous differential equations was integrated by numerical methods on a Univac 1108 computer using the Runge-Kutta integration technique. For ten days of hourly simulation, 42 seconds of computer time was necessary.

IRRIGATION

The opportunities that the computer affords the planner and the manager in the area of irrigation do not differ in essence from those in the other areas surveyed in this book. Before the advent of the computer, studies had to be restricted in general to single crop systems. The computer has made it possible to deal with the large number of state variables involved in multi-crop, multi-soil systems. A typical example is the optimization of a multi-crop (corn and soybean), multi-soil farm irrigation system in a humid area, where irrigation is necessary during brief but severe drought periods [20]. To deal with the large number of variables, the example uses a two-level optimization scheme which decomposes the irrigation system into smaller subsystems (individual acre unit crop-soil combinations) to be optimized separately before optimizing the entire system. The first level of optimization employs dynamic programming which is well suited to multi-stage decision processes and can handle the uncertain nature of weather elements (generated through a stochastic program based on a hydrologic record for rainfall and evaporation). The second level employs instead linear programming, to select the optimal crop mix, the level and extent of irrigation development and the type of irrigation system which will yield the maximum profit within the system constraints (on the basis of data obtained from studies of costs and labor requirements for irrigation and additional fertilizer, seeds, spray, etc.).

PROCESS CONTROL

URBAN WATER SUPPLY

Several major features characterize a comprehensive process control system for urban water supply:

- Automatic remote control of pumping units and major valves, to minimize operating personnel and achieve better coordination throughout the system
- Data transmission to a central location, for recording and use in system operation
- Centrally controlled office, to electronically scan and log pertinent requested information
- Ability to run the water supply system in a closed loop operation with the computer, to yield maximum system efficiency with minimum operating cost.

An example of the level of monitoring and total operational control that can be found in a complex water distribution system is given by the Denver Water Supply System [21]. Although the system used initially a gravity feed scheme, currently 53% of the water must be pumped by means of a system that includes 26 pump stations and 23 pressure zones. All pump stations were automated during the 1950's and additional controls were added in the distribution system. The system has been developed in three phases. Phase I, the "Power Conservation Phase," received its name from the calculated predictions that the computer-controlled pumps and other related equipment would consume less total power because their operational time was optimized. A DEC PDP-8 digital computer with approximately 8,000 words of core memory and 33,000 words of disc storage was installed for this purpose. Programming an alarm output was accomplished with an ASR-33 Teletype and two IBM Models. The experience in Phase I showed that to keep installation costs at a minimum, it is desirable to select a single manufacturer for all equipment, thereby reducing the necessity to purchase interconnecting equipment.

Phase II, the "Load Shifting Phase," initiated in 1970, had the main purpose of developing the ability to input field data directly into the computer. Generally, this was accomplished by monitoring the pressures of distribution zones and the valve positions at the supply end of these zones.

Phase III, the "Total Demand Phase," currently in progress, involves coupling the computer with the logger, and programming the computer to operate the distribution system facilities. Because of the many pressure zones that must be monitored, the execution of this phase is time consuming and expected to require from three to five years from its inception. Plans for a fourth phase include automatic operation of filter plants from the distribution network, control of the operation of distant water collection facilities (125-150 miles from the city), and the bringing of the entire system under automatic or computer control.

OPERATION OF DISTRIBUTION SYSTEMS

As in other process control applications, one of the major initial considerations in the use of a digital computer in the operation of a distribution network is the proper choice of computer size and type, the requirements for application to a particular job, and the ability of the computer to handle future growth [22]. This must be done in terms of present and future usage, because often costs over a period of years are less if expensive add-ons are avoided by initially purchasing a computer with greater capabilities. If a water process control computer is contemplated to replace an existing and less adequate one, several economic factors must be considered, including: initial cost of the new system, cost for conversion, operational and maintenance costs, useful life, and cost to expand the old system.

An example of the evolution of a computer-assisted water distribution system is given by the Monore County Water Authority [23]. The Authority supplies over 300,000 people in 13 towns and 2 villages, and in part of the City of Rochester. Because of geographical conditions, the Authority must operate some 23 booster pumping stations and 28 elevated tanks and standpipes (some at present still planned our under construction) and a 50,000,000 gallon reservoir. Since 1963, a telemetering system had been used by the Authority with manually operated pump controls. In 1966, an IBM 1130 computer was employed for billing and distribution network analyses, but by 1968, because of increased work load on the computer and employees, the expansion of operations was taken under consideration. After a thorough investigation, an IBM 1800 data acquisition and control system was selected to replace the IBM 1130. The IBM 1800 system had 32,000 words of storage capacity and required 2 μsec for access to memory. It had a multiple-programming operating system (MPX), with the capability of handling more than one program simultaneously (one running program could be interrupted and a program of higher priority run in its place). The IBM 1800 was selected because it could handle commercial functions while aiding in system control. Although the existing IBM 1130 system could be expanded at less cost than the proposed 1800 system, it did not have process control capability and was, therefore, eliminated from consideration. The useful life of the 1800 system was assessed to exceed 4½ years, a figure which made it more economical to purchase than to rent.

After sufficient time for entering and checking commercial programs has elapsed, process control equipment was added. Control programs entered into the computer include programs for:

- File maintenance
- System maintenance
- Diagnostic scheduling and updating
- Report record keeping
- Interface inquiry
- Main-lining.

Main-line programs are the most essential to automated system control. In operating a booster pumping station, for example, a mainline program takes into account date, time, tank level, suction and discharge pressures and pump running hours. The value of the computer becomes readily apparent from a calculation of the cumulative time—for all stations in the system— necessary for the operators to accumulate and record the corresponding data and to make decisions.

The report and inquiry programs serve to provide hourly reports on the status of major booster stations, of all storage facilities, and of other booster stations that are in operation. At the beginning of each 8 hour shift a report is generated to give the status of the entire system's function. Inquiry programs allow the operator to check the entire status of all facilities in any one of six areas sectioned according to method of operation, location of facilities, and pressure zones.

By using the computer for system control, savings were anticipated in total power consumption, maintenance, problem evaluation, and personnel utilization. Projected 10% annual savings in power consumption alone are expected to pay for the computer and the commercial functions equipment. The computer can also more easily handle difficult operating conditions; for instance, changing valve settings to raise or lower the pressures at booster stations and throughout the transmission mains can be done more accurately, thus alleviating the sometimes dangerous nature of this operation. The authority hopes in the future to add dynamic network analysis to the control system, so as to make it possible to analyze the distribution system under dynamic conditions.

The San Antonio Water Board provides another significant example of the use of computers in the operation of a water distribution system. The Board operates one of the major water systems in the United States [24]. The water production and distribution system, completely automated by 1963, was put under computer control in 1966. During the first year of computer operation, emergency maintenance was reduced by 10%. While monitoring water production, distribution, and storage, the computer analyzes the data and gives direct commands through telemetered signals to activate valves and pumps at two major pumping stations. Six other primary pumping stations, 13 elevated storage tanks, 32 secondary pumping stations and 8 booster stations are operated remotely from the central station. Since 1968, the computerized water distribution system has been integrated with a closed loop control system computer, operated to supply civic and industrial customers with chilled water for air conditioning and steam for heating. The control systems center now scans 180 points (representing 350 variables) every 15 milliseconds. Plans include future operation of an "on-line" process computer with another computer system to perform customer billing and various municipal applications.

Looking at the future, it is clear that with customer data on hand, computer analyses on an hourly basis can be of maximum usefulness in determining storage withdrawal and in projecting when storage and pumping facilities would be needed. The computer can also improve customer billing data which, once compiled, can be used directly as inputs to a network analysis.

WATER TREATMENT – THE CHICAGO FILTRATION PLANT

Its size and complexity make the Chicago Treament Plant an important example of computer process control in water treatment [24]. Occupying 61 acres, with a maximum capacity of 1.7 billion gallons per day, and serving a population of 2,700,000 in Chicago as well as 36 suburban communities, the plant was reorganized recently to incorporate computer control. The computer, an IBM 1800, performs scanning, logging and correlation of performance data (utilizing 205 analog and 106 contact-type input signals), and converts them into readily usable forms for "off-line" analysis. The computer also monitors plant operations, activiates alarms, and computes and paces chemical dosages. For example, 81 chemical flow measurements are required for application of 7 chemicals at 63 potential points. At an early stage of development, control loops were closed on some chemical feeding points while other direct control processes were left out of the system design; the system thus represents a hybrid configuration of both "on-line" and "off-line" process control (see Chapter IV).

SEWAGE TREATMENT PLANTS

The use of the digital computers in the operation and control of treatment plants, although quite recent, is becoming standard practice. Automatic monitor and control of sewage treatment plant operation can include [25]:

- Computer-assisted plant reporting
- Automated instrumentation
- Statistical data analysis
- Mathematical modeling
- Programmed digester control
- Flow control.

Characteristic examples of process control are given by the Arakawa [26] and Franklin [27] treatment plants. At the Arakawa plant computer functions are assigned on three levels:

- Normal — data acquisition and process status
- Optimizing — setpoint instructions for relay pump station control, air control, and return sludge control
- Management — correlation analysis, control prediction, and operational decisions.

To provide the data necessary for these functions, 845 digital communications channels link the CPU (32K) and supporting facilities (512K magnetic drum, line printer, typewriters, video displays) to the equipment controlling the operation. For ease of control, emphasis has been placed on the man-machine interaction by incorporating extensive use of the CRT to display warnings, trends, operational guides, etc.

The Franklin Treatment Plant and the Miami Conversancy District (MCD) exemplify the systems approach to computer control [28]. The MCD operates a comprehensive river basin program including water quality management, flood control, and water supply, and is the result of local initiative on the part of the industries and municipalities [27]. In December 1973 MCD was about to let a contract to Modular Computer Corporation (Mod Comp) for a computer to be located at the Franklin Treatment Plant, and for another at the MCD office. The Mod Comp II model 25 computer (16K, 1M. disc, CRT, teletype) located at Franklin will serve as a dedicated process control computer for the treatment plant. It will monitor power usage, DO, pH, solids and other parameters, and by means of set point optimization and direct digital control it will turn on aerators, pump sludge, etc. Data, status reports, and alarm conditions will be transmitted via a dedicated line to the Mod Comp II model 25 computer (32K, 5M. disc, CRT, teletype, card reader, lineprinter, tape) located at the MCD office. The office, which is designed to handle some seven plants, will supervise the plant. Approximately 95% of the ADP activities at MCD are engineering activities, with plant supervision time estimated at 1% day/plant. Other activities include water quality and precipitation studies, analysis and design of flood control facilities, flood control simulation, and the maintenance of a data bank, with data based, in part, on 6 Schneider Robot monitors. This overall systems approach toward the river basin incorporates all the facets — data collection, analysis, and control — required to effectively manage a water resource.

REFERENCES

[1]   McPherson, M.B. and Radziul, J.B., Water Distribution Design and the McIlroy Network Analyzer, *Journal of the Hydraulics Division*, ASCE, 84, 1958, 1588-1-19.

[2]   Graves, Q.B. and Branscome, B., Digital Computers for Pipeline Network Analysis, *Journal of the Sanitary Engineering Division*, ASCE, 84, 1958, 1608-1-18.

[3]   Sinkoff, M.D., Geilker, C.D., and Rennerfelt, J.G., An Analog Computer for the Oxygen Sag Curve, *Journal of The Sanitary Engineering Division*, ASCE, 84, 1958, 1850-1-8.

[4]   Brock, D.A., Closed-Loop Automatic Control of Water System Operations, *Journal of the American Water Works Association*, 55, 1963, 467-480.

[5]   Shirley, W.O. and Bailey, J.J., Use of Digital Comptuers in Distribution System Analyses, *Journal of the American Water Works Association*, 58, 1966, 1575-1584.

[6]   Deb. A.K. and Sarkar, A.I., Optimization in Design of Hydraulic Network, *Journal of the Sanitary Engineering Division*, ASCE, 97, 1971, 141-159.

[7]   Wu, L.C., *Design of Optimal Water Distribution Networks Using Dynamic Programming*, Report UMICH-ENVSA-71-6, University of Michigan, School of Public Health, July 1971, 20 pp.

[8]   Hsu, J.S. and Deininger, R.A., *A Minimum Cost Water Distribution Network*, Report UMICH-ENVASA-71-04, University of Michigan, School of Public Health, June 1971, 17 pp.

[9]   Kally, E., Computerized Planning of the Least Cost Water Distribution Network, *Water and Sewage Works*, 119, 1972, R-121-127.

[10] Carlson, T.J., Hsu, J.S., and Deininger, R.A., *An Interactive Design System for Water Distribution Networks*, Report UMICH-ENVASA-71-5, University of Michigan, School of Public Health, July 1971, 9 pp.

[11] Engineering News-Record, All Alternatives Explored as Computer Refines Sewer Designs, *Engineering News-Record*, 178, 1967, 43-44.

[12] Merritt, L.B. and Bogan, R.H., Computer-Based Optimal Design of Sewer Systems, *Journal of the Environmental Engineering Division*, ASCE, 99, 1973, 35-53.

[13] DeGroat, J.J., Pomeroy, B.A., and Hagadorn, R.E., Computer Design of Sewage Treatment Plants, *Public Works*, 101, 1970, 51-53.

[14] DeGroat, J.J., personal communications, President, Technicomp, Inc., Great Neck, New York, 1973.

[15] Norris, R., personal communications, Director of Computer Applications, Quirk, Lawler and Matusky, Tappan, New York, 1973.

[16] Koenig, L., Optimal Fail-Safe Process Design, *Journal Water Pollution Control Federation*, 44, 1972, 1718-1729.

[17] American Association of Professors of Sanitary Engineering, Applications of Analog Computers in Sanitary Engineering, *Proceedings*, 3rd Annual Workshop, June 1968.

[18] Burkhead, C.E. and Wood, D.J., Analog Simulation of Activated Sludge Systems, *Journal of the Sanitary Engineering Division*, ASCE, 95, 1969, 593-606.

[19] Chen, C.W., Concepts and Utilities of Ecologic Model, *Journal of the Sanitary Engineering Division, ASCE*, 96, 1970, 1085-1097.

[20] Windsor, J.S. and Chow, V.E., Model for farm Irrigation in Humid Areas, *Journal of the Irrigation and Drainage Division*, ASCE, 97, 1971, 369-385.

[21] Carlson, C.E.C., The Denver System of Water Works Controls, *Journal of the American Water Works Assoication*, 63, 1971, 513-516.

[22] Neel, R.C., Computer Applications in Distribution, *Journal of the American Water Works Association*, 63, 1971, 485-489.

[23] Frenz, C.M., Automated System Control, *Journal of the American Water Works Association*, 63, 1971, 508-512.

[24] American Public Works Association Research Foundation, *Public Works Computer Applications*, Results of a Research Project Sponsored by Nineteen Local Governmental Agencies, August 1970.

[25] Koch M., Computer Control of Wastewater Treatment, *Journal Water Pollution Control Federation*, 44, 1972, 1718-1729.

[26] Tohyama, S., Computer Control — Arakawa Treatment Plant, *Water Research*, 6, 1972, 591-595.

[27] Heckroth, C.S., Cooperative Water Quality Effort Pays Off, *Water and Wastes Engineering*, 8, 6, 1971, 32-35, 53

[28] Whitaker, D., personal communications, ADP manager, Miami Conversancy District, Dayton, Ohio, 1973.

VIII. LOOKING TO THE FUTURE

In this final chapter we briefly summarize some of the major considerations and issues that have emerged in the previous chapters, and we recommend to the decision-maker in water resources appropriate actions in the areas of most urgent need.

The advent of the computer has provided water resources technology with a complex, tripartite system consisting of (1) hardware, or the computer itself and related equipment; (2) software, or the languages needed to communicate with the computer; and (3) methodologies, or the computational and logical protocols and approaches that one must use to take advantage of the capabilities of the computer. Hardware and software together form a computer system; software and appropriate methodologies form the user's programs. There are trends and issues of great impact on water resources technology in each of these areas, as well as in their interactions.

While some of these trends and issues are more conveniently viewed under the general terms of hardware, software, and methodology, others are better discussed by focusing on some of the major areas of application of computers to water resources, such as data acquisition and management, process control, and system analysis and design.

COMPUTER AREAS

HARDWARE

The first major issue concerning hardware is the degree to which centralized systems should be developed. These systems, in their fullest form, consist of computer utilities with associated libraries, data banks, programming staffs, and peripheral support equipment. A number of questions regarding such centralization need to be resolved. For example:

- Should there be dedicated computer utilities devoted exclusively to water resources systems?
- Can the needs of water resources systems be satisfied by the more generalized, multi-purpose computer utilities currently extant?

162

Before decisions on such issues can be made, there is a need for systematic analysis of the formatting and documentation problems involved in structuring a utility, the cost and economic constraints of such a system, as well as of the role of program libraries, data banks, programming staffs, etc. within the utility.

A second issue is how to reorient the user in the water resources field to the changes that will be brought about by the rapid introduction and diffusion of minicomputers. We have seen that one of the most significant effects of the advent of minicomputers is the breaking loose of the organizational structure under which computers have been operating. This will inevitably lead to a de-emphasis of computer centers, unless such systems are part of extensive computer utilities. A concomitant issue concerns data and computational management—that is, the extent to which data and programs should be stored and operated on at a user site or at a centralized utility. Thus, the advent of minicomputers cannot be dissociated from the issue of the proper organization of a computer utility.

A third major issue arises from the development of intimately connected computer-instrument packages, now made possible by inexpensive logic and memory elements. What is the optimum interface between sensors and data processing and logic decision-making systems? It is clear that such an interface no longer needs to be rigidly designed. The capabilities introduced by the minicomputer make it possible to consider a system with multiple levels of data processing, as well as to assign to hardware some of the tasks that were exclusively carried out by software in traditional computer installations.

From a policy viewpoint, there is an urgent need for systematic technico-economic studies of the optimum interface. There is an equal need to analyze each component of water resources systems, to determine the instrumentation requirements that would best facilitate the analysis and control functions, and to assess the extent to which the combination of computers and sensors could best serve the purpose.

An interesting hardware consideration arises in connection with hybrid computer systems. These systems provide much greater flexibility and speed than the purely digital ones and have come to replace, in most areas of technology, the exclusively analog systems. In almost every area of water resources, analog systems, initially predominant, have yielded to digital ones. Yet the analog approach offers, in a number of cases, considerable advantage over the digital; a hybrid system makes it possible to utilize the best of both approaches. In general, the introduction of hybrid systems appears to be particularly desirable in the preliminary phases of planning, design, and analysis, where rapid focusing on a "first-cut" solution is sought. It is also desirable in the area of process control as well as in a number of other specialized applications. Yet, as of now, hybrid systems have been incorporated into the field of water resources only to a very limited degree. The question is whether this is a vicious circle, stemming from relative unfamiliarity with hybrid systems, and from the abandonment of hybrid facilities and instruction in most engineering schools.

SOFTWARE

As size, speed and complexity of computer systems increase, the creation of effective user-machine interfaces becomes ever more critical. Appropriate software must be developed and managed, in conjunction with appropriate hardware. By far the least recognized and most costly of the problems is the lack of software engineering and management in water resources technology. Establishment of rational and systematic procedures is essential if the cost of programming is to be reduced and the effectiveness of software enhanced.

A second problem is how to facilitate the user's approach to the computer. Two tasks are involved: 1) to facilitate the user's ability to write, initiate and run programs and to receive understandable outputs, and 2) to improve the user's understanding of the structure of computer language and of how a computer program accomplishes a given task. The construction of plotters and highly interactive graphic display systems as well as the development of high level languages represent significant steps forward. However, despite the current advances in techniques such as image processing and artificial intelligence, the problem is far from having been solved.

A third software problem is how to facilitate communication between users, to provide a given user with the benefit of another user's experience in approaching a similar problem. There is a need for a policy aimed at encouraging such a communication—a policy that must inevitably consider the issue of establishing certain standards for communication. Communication between users can also be enhanced by creating program libraries and problem-oriented languages, all of which lead in turn to certain standards of programming and documentation, and, therefore, facilitate communication. Clearly, libraries and problem-oriented languages not only involve issues in software, but also demand a review of problem-solving methodologies, and need to be flexible enough to accommodate the continuous evolution of such methodologies.

METHODOLOGY

The introduction of the computer has greatly heightened the need for continued development of appropriate methodologies for analysis, planning, design, and operation of water resources systems. Most of the present approaches have evolved from what was essentially a computerization of methods originally developed for hand calculation, to approaches more appropriate for the computer (such as stochastic ones, various methods for solving differential equations, and process control approaches). However, these developments have not occurred uniformly throughout the field; furthermore, only seldom have the characteristics of the computer system to be used—both hardware and software—been taken systematically into account. For instance, still largely unexplored is the issue of whether or not access to appropriate data banks may introduce greater sophistication in water resources technology. (The banks might contain data about the natural environment, the hydrologic environment, soil conditions, etc., as well as appropriate design, economic, and sociological data.) Currently, the major methodological difficulties in the planning of water resources systems arise not as much in dealing with the physical aspects of the system, as in dealing with the economic and socio-political ones; it is particularly in these areas that appropriate methodologies and data banks are needed.

A corollary issue in the area of methodology is whether a substantial amount of public efforts should be invested in the development of master, generalized, computer programs with appropriate flexibility, capable of solving major types of water resources problems e.g., the modeling of the BOD in a body of water or the planning of a multiple-purpose system of reservoirs, or the optimal control of a generalized groundwater system. The alternative is the continuation of the present approach whereby specific problems are solved 'ad hoc' by each user (an approach, it should be noted, more the result of a lack of policy than of any deliberate program of action). Establishment of a policy governing the development of major computer programs would require ample consultations with the users in the field, and with the producers of software, hardware, and programs.

APPLICATION AREAS

DATA ACQUISITION AND MANAGEMENT

The computer has drastically altered the process of data acquisition and management for water resources systems—probably the single greatest contribution of the computer to water resources technology. One of the most complex issues arising in this context is that as the size and scope of water resource problems and models increase, the researcher and the practitioner must rely ever more on data collection agencies, particularly when lengthy historical records and numerous sociological factors must be considered. The efficiency with which these data agencies respond to the needs of the community of users comes to exert a major influence on the users. There are of course hardware questions that arise in the operation of any such agency (such as equipment size and flexibility), but they are overshadowed by software questions, such as what format to use for the data and how to best manage the overall system—how to best collect, catalogue, document, check and finally disseminate vast amounts of data in a timely fashion.

Several trends and factors—in part overlapping with areas already discussed, but worth reiterating—will influence future activities in data acquisition and management:

- The use of minicomputers and microcomputers as front-end processors, in both centralized and isolated configurations
- The use of computer-instrument packages, to provide data more rapidly or to provide data that were not previously available
- The ability to develop more integrated data collection and dissemination systems
- The increased flexibility and capabilities of centralized data systems, made possible by the advent of computers with virtual memory
- The guidance procedures and methods for collecting, documenting, and disseminating computer programs, ensuing from the growing development of program libraries and program indices
- The increasingly favorable economics of centralized facilities, as the result of greater speeds of communications equipment and of the increasing use of teleprocessing
- The ability to receive large amounts of data in a form directly compatable with the user's computer, thus reducing or eliminating the need for human intervention.

ANALYSIS AND DESIGN

Analysis and design encompass a very broad spectrum of activities that lie between data collection and process control; most work in this area results in "programs," that tend to be more machine independent than those characteristic of data and process control systems. The trends of major significance are, on the one hand, the increasing use of computer-generated designs and of interactive approaches and, on the other hand, the development of increasingly powerful algorithms such as dynamic programming or finite element methods.

PROCESS CONTROL

Most of the current research in process control instrumentation is seeking to develop new and more accurate automatic sensors for pertinent parameters such as flow rates, bacterial content, temperature, or volatile acids in waste. Digital devices, particularly minicomputers, with their ability to preprocess data and program an instrument or device, are bound to exert a revolutionary influence on the future methodology of process control. Most minicomputers can be easily interfaced with external hardware, so that the process of connecting sensors and controllers generally does not present a formidable task. When the decision-making segment of a process control system is straightforward, the minicomputer introduces a utilization factor far superior to that of larger computer systems. The problem of maintenance—a major one when control systems are distributed over large areas and varying environmental conditions—also can be reduced by minicomputers of modular construction.

There is still considerable reluctance to installing process controllers in a number of specific water resources systems and subsystems. The reluctance stems primarily from issues in the areas of communications, computers, and system models, and indicates that the problem must be approached not only in terms of what is technologically possible (and many process control systems hardly use "state of the art" technology), but rather from the application viewpoint. For instance:

- What effect do downtime failures have on the system?
- Have the problems that process control present in manpower, training of personnel, etc. been analyzed?
- Has the system been adequately modeled, so that the number and placement of sensors within the system provide the data necessary to control the system?

These factors often play a more important role than equipment capability in deciding on a process control system. Finally, it is important to stress again that, to date, the digital computer appears to be most apt for complex process control applications, and is used much more extensively than either the analog or the hybrid. However, with more research and exposure, the hybrid computer may offer distinct advantages and come to be more widely used.

THE OVERALL ISSUE

The problems and trends we have just discussed can be viewed as facets of an overall issue: *whether there should be national and possibly international strategies governing the use of computers in water resources.* Wide-spread lack of awareness of the complex dimensions of the impact of computers on water resources technology, and the fragmentation of computer usage among a myriad of water resources agencies, organizations and individuals, have been without doubt a major obstacle to the establishment of guidelines or agreements. It appears highly desirable that efforts be made toward the establishment of such guidelines or agreements in brief, toward the establishment of a comprehensive computer strategy for water resources.

In addition to the specific issues outlined earlier in this chapter, the questions to be considered in assessing the possible elements of such a strategy should include:

- The overall level of resources to be devoted to the evolution of hardware, software, and methodologies for water resources.
- The responsibilities of various government levels and agencies for a more effective use of computer systems. For instance, should a computer program be considered a capital improvement and amortized as such (a measure that would greatly encourage the development of quality software and of a corresponding industry)? Should major computer programs be rated as to computational efficacy or some other appropriate parameter? Should national or international agencies make use of their consolidated buying power to channel into a given direction, hardware and software developments in water resources?
- The establishment of measures aimed at giving users and decision-makers at all levels appropriate education concerning the issues discussed in this book. This appears to be a glaring and expensive omission today, particularly in view of the fact that computer costs are, to a large extent, software costs, which in turn are greatly affected by a large number of parameters. To provide water resource personnel with some basic skills in programming is simply not sufficient. An understanding of

software engineering and of the other issues we have reviewed, is essential for rational and cost-effective use of computers.

THE STRUCTURE OF THE INTERFACE BETWEEN COMPUTER SYSTEMS AND WATER RESOURCES TECHNOLOGY

A proper policy is bound to lead to an increasingly rational structuring of the interface between users and computer systems in water resources technology. The principal elements of such a structure, some of which are already in existence to various degrees of development, are bound to include:

- *National (and at times international) networks of computers,* to provide the user in the water resources field with large amounts of computer power. Although at present there is no substantial computer network dedicated solely to water resources, there are already in existence other networks, such as the ARPA network in the United States, that could be used, in part, for this field.

- *National (and at times international) networks of communications,* to allow the data necessary for the analysis, planning, and operation of water resource systems to be easily communicated between the elements of the systems. Here again the issue is the extent to which the water resources field, in the long run, will require its own communication networks, or will be able to use networks established for other purposes, such as the digital network that may be established by the U.S. Post Office for electronically transmitting mail, or the Bell System network.

- *Data banks for the storage, management and dissemination of information.* These banks are exemplified at this moment by those established in the United States by the Geological Survey and the Environmental Protection Agency.

- *Information acquisition systems,* to collect data for data banks and other elements of water resource systems. At present, the most technically advanced component of such a system are satellites, such as ERTS-1; computer-instrument packages are another advanced element which is beginning to emerge. More traditional elements of the system have been in operation for a long time, but do not have the global capability of the satellites or the versatility of networks with computer-instrument packages.

- *Program libraries* for the collection, maintenance, and dissemination (often through computers and communications networks) of programs of widespread usefulness in water resources technology. Current examples include the library collected by the Hydrologic Engineering Center of the U.S. Corps of Engineers, the HYDRO Library, and the computerized procedures of the Hydraulic Design Manual of the U.S. Waterways Experiment Station.

- *A set of problem-oriented computer languages,* to facilitate the user's approach to the computer and the construction of large computer programs. While currently there are no problem-oriented computer languages for water resources which are operational, there are significant examples of such languages which have been developed primarily for educational and demonstrational purposes, such as HYDRO and HYDRA-FORTRAN.

- *Diversified, flexible and powerful process control systems,* making it possible to control, in part or totally, a water resources system. While process control can occur at a multiplicity of levels, at present process control on a large scale is non-existent, and process control for the smaller water resource systems or components is also far from being adequately developed.

Other desirable elements of the computer-water resources system interface will undoubtedly emerge in the future. They may include mechanisms (e.g., centers) for the encouragement and development of increasingly powerful modeling, design, and operational methodologies, mechanisms for policy studies on the most desirable role of the computer and on how to attain it, and mechanisms for the technological forecasting of future impacts of computers on water resources technology. Many of these elements can greatly benefit from connection to supranational mechanisms, exemplified by the World Weather Watch Program, a global data processing and telecommunications system established by the World Meteorological Organization [1].

REFERENCES

[1]   *The Application of Computer Technology for Development,* United Nations Publication, No. E. 71. II. A. 1, 1971, pp. 37-38.

APPENDICES

A1. COMMERCIALLY AVAILABLE MINICOMPUTERS

(adapted from Chapter II [11])

"The following charts list the most important features of 68 minicomputer models. For the purposes of this survey, a minicomputer is defined as a system which, in a minimum configuration of processor, power supply, terminal interface and 4k-words of memory, costs less than $20,000. Because of this definition, several manufacturers (IBM, Cascade Data, Eldorado Electrodata, and others) were not included. These manufacturers produce computers which, although sometimes classified as minicomputers, more properly belong in the class of small systems. In the survey listings, where an asterisk (*) appears next to a model name this indicates that the model listed is representative of two or more essentially similar systems. Unlisted models are often either ruggedized or OEM versions of the listed model." Reprinted from COMPUTER DECISIONS, October, 1972, Copyright 1972, Hayden Publishing Company.

Company	Model	Word length (bits)/Instruction length	Times (microsec.) Cycle/Add	Word capacity min.-max.	Hardware (standard)	Software features	Price: 4k/8k
Bendix	BDX9000*	16	1.0 / 2.0	4k to 32k	M-D, PF	2-pass	$6,000 / —
Cincinnati Milacron	CIP/2100*	8 / 8/16	1.1 / 6.38	4k to 32k	M-D, DMA	2-pass	$4,565 / $4,865
Clary Datacomp	404	16 / 16/32	2.2 / 9.8	1k to 65k	M-D	1-pass, RPGII, Basic	$7,000 / $9,000
Computer Automation	Alpha 16*	16 / 16	1.6 / 3.2	2k to 32k	M-D, DMA	1-2-pass, Fortran, Basic	$3,550 / $4,750
	Alpha 8*	16 / 16	1.6 / 3.2	4k to 32k	DMA	1+2-pass	$2,800 / $3,300
Control Data	1700	16+2 / 16/32	1.1 / 2.2	4k to 32k	M-D, PF, PC, SP	2-pass, Macro, Fortran	$20,000 / $26,500
	SC 1700	16+2 / 16/32	1.5 / 3.0	4k to 32k	PC, SP, M-D, PF	2-pass, Macro, Fortran	$15,900 / $20,400
Data General	Nova 1220*	16 / 16	1.2 / 1.35	1k to 64k	DMA	2-pass, Fortran, Algol, Basic	$5,250 / $6,650
	Nova 820	16 / 16	0.8 / 0.8	1k to 64k	DMA	2-pass, Fortran, Algol, Basic	$6,450 / $7,850
	Supernova	16 / 16	0.8 / 0.8	1k to 64k	DMA	Same as above	$9,600 / $10,850
	Supernova SC	16 / 16	0.3/0.8 / 0.3/0.8	1k to 64k	DMA	Same as above	$14,250 / $15,500
Datacraft	6024/5	24 / 24	1.0 / 2.0	4k to 65k	PC, M-D	2-pass, Fortran, Macro, Basic, RPG, Snobol	$11,250 / —
Digital Computer Controls	D-112	12 / 12/24	1.2 / 2.4	4k to 32k	SP	1-2-pass, Macro, Fortran, Algol, Basic	$3,490 / $4,550

Manufacturer	Model	Word length	Instr.	Cycle time	Memory	Features	Software	Price	Price
	D-112H	12	12/24	0.2/0.9; 2.4	256 to 32k	SP	1+2-pass, Macro, Fortran, Algol, Basic	$4,095	$5,150
	D-116	16	16	1.2; 1.35	2k to 32k	PF, DMA	2-pass, Macro, Fortran, Algol, Basic	$4,000	$5,400
Digital Equipment	PDP-8/E*	12	12/24	1.2; 2.6	4k to 32k	DMA	1+2-pass, Macro, Fortran, Algol, Basic, Focal	$4,490	$5,650
	PDP-8/F*	12	12/24	1.2; 2.6	4k to 16k	—	Same as above	$3,990	$5,150
	PDP-11/10*	16	16/32/48	1.2; 2.3	4k to 32k	PF, DMA	2-pass, Fortran, Basic	—	$6,995
	PDP-11/20*	16	16/32/48	0.9; 2.3	4k to 124k	PF, DMA	2-pass, Fortran, Macro, Basic	$9,300	$12,900
	PDP-11/40	16	16/32/48	0.9; 2.3	8k to 124k	SP, DMA	Same as above	—	$12,995
	PDP-11/45	16	16/32/48	0.85; 2.3	4k to 124k	SP, M-D, PF, DMA	Same as above	$14,990	—
Electronic Associates	Pacer	16	16	1.0; 2.0	8k to 32k	SP, M-D, PF	2-pass, Fortran	—	$15,200
Electronic Processors	EPI-118	18	18	0.9; 2.0	4k to 32k	SP, PF	2-pass, Macro, Basic	$2,790	$3,990
	EPI-218	18	18/36	0.9; 2.0	4k to 32k	SP, PF, DMA	2-pass, Basic	$3,490	—
Four-Phase	System IV/70	24	24	2.0; 16	4k to 32k	PF, DMA PC, M-D	2-pass, Cobol	$16,000	$22,600
Fujitsu	Facom U-200	16-2	16/32	0.65; 1.5	4k to 65k	PC, PF, DMA	2-pass, Macro, Fortran	$8,500	$10,600
General Automation	SPC-12*	8	8/16	2.16; 6.48	4k to 16k	—	1-pass	$2,980	$3,980

Code: PC = parity checking; SP = storage protection; M-D = hardware multiply-divide; FP = hardware floating point; PF = power failure protection; DMA = direct memory access channel; * = other similar models available.

Company	Model	Word length (bits)/Instruction length	Times (microsec.) Cycle/Add	Word capacity min.-max.	Hardware (standard)	Software features	Price: 4k/8k
General Automation	SPC-16	16	0.8/1.4	4k to 65k	PF, DMA	1-pass, Macro, Fortran, others	$3,950 / $5,350
	System 18/30	16 / 16/32	0.96 / 2.4	4k to 32k	PC, SP, M-D, PF, DMA	2-pass, Macro, Fortran, others	$18,000 / $23,000
General Electric	3010/2	16 / 16/32	1.0 / 1.0	4k to 32k	M-D, FP, DMA	1, 2, or 3-pass, Fortran	$10,900 / $14,500
GRI	99/30*	16 / 16	1.76 / 0.9/1.76	4k to 32k	M-D, FP, DMA	2-pass	$3,740 / $5,100
GTE	Tempo 2*	16 / 16/32	0.75 / 1.5	4k to 65k	PF, DMA	2-pass, Macro, Fortran	$5,700 / $7,500
Hewlett-Packard	2100A*	16 / 16	0.98 / 1.96	4k to 32k	PC, SP, M-D, PF	2-pass, Fortran, Algol, Basic	$6,900 / $10,400
Honeywell	316*	16 / 16	1.6 / 3.2	4k to 32k	—	1+2-pass, Fortran, Macro, Basic	$8,400 / $11,900
	700	16	0.77 / 1.55	8k to 32k	PF, DMA	2-pass, Fortran, Macro, Basic	— / $19,400
Intel	MCS-8*	8 / 8/16/24	10 / 10 to 20	256 to 16k	—	2-pass	$900 / $1,400
Interdata	Model 55*	16 / 16/32	1.0	4k to 32k	FP, PF, M-D, DMA	1+2-pass, Fortran, Basic, RTOS	— / $15,900
	Model 70*	16 / 16/32	1.0	4k to 32k	M-D, FP, DMA	1+2-pass, Fortran, Basic, RTOS	$6,800 / $9,500
	Model 80	16 / 16/32	0.24 / 0.45	8k to 32k	M-D, FP, DMA	1+2-pass, Fortran, Basic, RTOS	— / $14,900
Lockheed	Mac Jr.	16 / 16	1.0 / 2.0	4k to 32k	—	2-pass, Macro, Fortran	$6,500 / $8,750
	Sue-1110	16 / 16/32	0.85/0.2 / 2.79	4k to 82k	PF, DMA	1-pass, Macro, Fortran, RPG II	$3,895 / $5,495

	Model								Price	
Microdata	Micro 400	8	8/16	1.6	1.6	1k to 65k	—	2-pass	$3,195	$4,690
	Micro 800	8	16	1.1	0.22	0 to 32k	—	2-pass	$4,875	$5,875
	Micro 810*	8	8/16/24/32	1.1	11	4k to 32k	—	2-pass, Basic	$5,875	$6,875
	Micro 1600*	8	8/16	1.0	0.2	0 to 65k	PF, DMA	2-pass	$4,995	$5,745
Modular	Modcomp I*	16	16/32	0.8	0.8	512 to 32k	DMA	2-pass	$4,400	$6,200
	Modcomp III*	16	16/32	0.8	0.8	4k to 65k	PC, PF	2-pass, Fortran, Basic	$9,850	$11,650
Nuclear Data	ND 812	12	12/24	2.0	4	4k to 16k	M-D, PF, DMA	2-pass	$6,950	$9,600
Prime	Prime 200	16	64	0.75	1.5	8k to 32k	DMA, PC	2-pass, Macro, Fortran, RTOS	—	$7,100
Omnus	Omnus 1	16	16/32	1.2	2.4	2k to 131k	PF, DMA	1+2-pass, Fortran	$6,500	$9,950
Quantel	Answer	8	24/48	1.5	57.5	4k to 32k	M-D, DMA	2-pass	$12,315	$14,465
Raytheon	704*	16	16	1.0	2.0	4k to 32k	—	1+2-pass, Macro, Fortran	$7,200	$9,200
Rolm	Ruggednova	16	16	2.6	5.9	256 to 32k	PF, DMA	2-pass, Fortran, Algol, Basic	$13,500	$19,500
SYS	1500*	8	24	0.5	0.5	512 to 65k	SP, PF, DMA	None	$1,500	—
Systems	Systems 71*	16	16	0.85	3	8k to 65k	SP, PF	1-pass, Fortran, Basic	—	$15,000
Texas Instruments	960A	16	32	0.75	3.2	4k to 65k	PC, SP, PF, DMA	2-pass, Macro, Fortran	$2,850	$4,350

Code: PC = parity checking; **SP** = storage protection; **M-D** = hardware multiply-divide; **FP** = hardware floating point; **PF** = power failure protection; **DMA** = direct memory access channel; * = other similar models available.

Company	Model	Word length (bits)	Instruction length	Times (microsec.) Cycle	Times (microsec.) Add	Word capacity min.–max.	Hardware (standard)	Software features	Price: 4k	Price: 8k
Texas Instruments	980A	16	16/32/48	0.75	0.75	4k to 65k	PC, SP, M-D, PF, DMA	2-pass Macro, Fortran	$3,475	$4,975
Unicom	CP-8	8	8/16	1.75	3.5	1k to 32k	—	2-pass	$3,400	$4,600
Unicomp	Comp-18	18	18	0.88	2.25	4k to 262k	PF, DMA	1+2-pass, Fortran, Basic	$11,000	$13,700
Varian	620/F-100	16	16/32	0.75	1.5	4k to 32k	SP, M-D, PF, DMA	2-pass, Fortran, Basic, RPG	$10,500	$13,000
	620/L*	16	16/32	1.8	3.6	4k to 32k	M-D, PF, DMA	Same as above	$5,400	$7,700
	620/L-100	16	16/32	0.95	1.9	4k to 32k	M-D, PF, DMA	Same as above	$6,400	$8,700
	V73	16	16	0.66	1.3	4k to 262k	PF, M-D, DMA	Macro and all above	$14,250	$16,250
Wang	3300	8	16	1.6	4.8	4k to 65k	PF, DMA	3-pass, Fortran, Basic	$4,950	$6,450
Westinghouse	2500	16	16	0.75	1.5	4k to 65k	M-D, PF	2-pass, Macro, Fortran, Basic, RPG	$9,950	$13,300
XLO	XLO-8	8	8/16	1.8	2.0	1k to 32k	—	2+3-pass	$4,200	$5,720

Code: PC = parity checking; SP = storage protection; M-D = hardware multiply-divide; FP = hardware floating point; PF = power failure protection; DMA = direct memory access channel; * = other similar models available.

A2. COMPUTER SYSTEMS AT SELECTED AGENCIES
(adapted from Chapter IV [5])

Agency	Model	Operating system	Memory size	Storage devices	Output devices
Agriculture					
ARS	IBM 360/30	OS	30K	Disc, tape, card.	Printer, tape.
FS	CDC 3100	MSOS 3	32K	Disc, tape.	Printer, tape.
	U 1108	Exec. 2	64K	Disc, tape.	Printer, tape.
SCS	IBM 360/65	OS	500K	Disc, tape, card.	Printer, card.
	IBM 1130	Ver 2 OS	8K	Disc, tape, card.	Printer, card.
Commerce					
EDS-NCC	RCA 70/45	TDOS	131K	Disc, tape.	Printer, tape, card.
NOS	IBM 360/30	DOS-100K	64K	Disc, tape.	Printer, tape.
NWS	IBM 1620	OS	20K	Card.	Printer (off-line), card.
	IBM 1130	OS	16K	Disc, card.	Printer, card.
	IBM 360/50	OS		Disc.	Printer, tape, card.
	CDC 3100	TOS	16K	Tape.	Printer, tape, card.
NMFS	IBM 1130		8K	Disc.	Printer.
Defense					
CE	RCA 301	TOS	40K	Tape.	Printer, tape, card.
	GE 225	Br. II	8K	Tape.	Printer, card.
	GE 427	DAPS	64K	Disc, tape.	Printer, card.
	GE 115	DAPS	4K	Disc, tape.	Printer, tape, card.
	GE 225	FIZMOP	16K	Tape, card.	Printer, tape, card, plotter.
	RCA		40K	Tape, card.	Printer, tape, card.
	GE 225	Fort IV	16K	Tape, card.	Printer, tape, card, plotter.
	IBM 360/30	TOS	32K	Tape.	Printer, card.
	IBM 1130		8K	Disc.	Printer, card.
	GE 225		8K	Tape.	Printer, card.
	GE 427	OS	32K		Printer.
	GE 425	TOS	64K	Disc.	Tape, card.
	GE 225	TOS	8K	Tape, card.	Printer, tape, card.
	GE 225	OS, TOS, DOS	8K	Tape.	Printer, card.
	CDC 6400		65K	Disc, tape.	Printer, plotter.
	IBM 7094	TOS			
	CDC 6600	TOS			
	IBM 360/50	OS	150K	Disc, tape.	
	IBM 360/50	OS	150K	Disc, tape.	Printer, card.
	IBM 360/50	OS	512K	Disc, tape.	Printer, card, teletype.
	IBM 1130	DOS	16K	Disc.	Printer, card, teletype.
	U 1108		265K	Drum, tape.	Printer.
	GE 225	TOS	16K	Tape, card.	Printer, plotter.

Agency	Model	Operating system	Memory size	Storage devices	Output devices
	GE 220		16K	Tape, card.	Printer, tape, card.
HEW					
PHS	H400	TOS	8K	Tape.	Printer, tape, card.
Interior					
BPA	CDC 6400	Scope 3.2	131K	Disc.	Printout.
BR	H 800/200	H	32K	Tape.	Printer, card.
	IBM 1620	Moniter 1	40K	Disc.	Printer, card, plotter.
	U 1108	Ex 8	132K	Drum.	Tape, plotter.
GS	IBM 360	OS	1000K	Disc, tape, card.	Printer, tape, card, plotter.
EPA-WPO	IBM 360	OS	1000K	Disc, tape.	Printer, tape, card, plotter, terminal.
TVA	IBM 360/50	OS	512K	Disc, tape.	Printer, tape, disc.
Non-Fed.					
Calif.	CDC 330		96K	Tape.	Printer, tape, plotter.
N.Y.	IBM 360/50				

A3. COMPUTER TERMINALS—USGS
(June 1973)

Responsible Division	Location	Make (Model #)	Speed
USGS Users			
Computer Cen.	Denver, Colorado	IBM (360-20)	H
Computer Cen.	Denver, Colorado	IBM (2741)	L
Computer Cen.	Flagstaff, Arizona	PDP 11	H
Computer Cen.	Flagstaff, Arizona	IBM (2741)	L
Computer Cen.	Menlo Park, California	Data 100 Corp.(78)	H
Computer Cen.	Menlo Park, California	IBM (2741)	L
Computer Cen.	Rolla, Missouri	IBM (360-20)	H
Computer Cen.	Int. Bldg., Wash., D.C.	IBM (2741)	L
Computer Cen.	Int. Bldg., Wash., D.C.	IBM (2741)	L
Computer Cen.	Int. Bldg., Wash., D.C.	IBM (2741)	L
Computer Cen.	Int. Bldg., Wash., D.C.	IBM (2741)	L
Computer Cen.	Int. Bldg., Wash., D.C.	IBM (2741)	L
Computer Cen.	Int. Bldg., Wash., D.C.	IBM (2741)	L
Conservation	New Orleans, Louisiana	Data 100 Corp.(78)	H
Conservation	Fort Worth, Texas	Data 100 Corp.(78)	H
Conservation	K St., N.W., Wash., D.C.	Data 100 Corp.(70)	H
Conservation	K St., N.W., Wash., D.C.	IBM (2741)	L
Conservation	GSA Bldg., Wash., D.C.	Teletype Corp.(33)	L
Geologic	NBS Bldg. 10., Wash., D.C.	Data 100 Corp(70)	H
Geologic	Silver Spring, Maryland	Memorex Corp. (1280)	H
Geologic	GSA Bldg., Wash., D.C.	Datel Corp. (30)	L
Geologic	Smithsonian Inst., Wash., D.C.	Novar Corp.(5-51)	L
Geologic	1717 H Street, Wash., D.C.	Teletype Corp.(33)	L
Geologic	Conn. Ave., Wash., D.C. (Old NBS)	Teletype Corp.(33)	L
Publications	GSA Bldg., Wash., D.C.	IBM Mag. Card	L
Topographic	McLean, Virginia	Data 100 Corp.(70)	H
Topographic	GSA Bldg., Wash., D.C.	Memorex Corp.(1280)	H
Topographic	McLean, Virginia	Teletype Corp.(33)	L
Water Res.	Arlington, Virginia	University Computing Co.	H
Water Res.	Bay St., Louis Miss (MTF)	Data 100 Corp.(78)	H
Water Res.	Portland, Oregon	Data 100 Corp.(74)	H
Water Res.	Atlanta, Georgia	Data 100 Corp.(70)	H
Water Res.	Atlanta, Georgia	Data 100 Corp.(70)	H
Water Res.	Baton Rogue, Louisiana	Data 100 Corp.(70)	H
Water Res.	Austin, Texas	Data 100 Corp.(70)	H
Water Res.	Garden Grove, California	Data 100 Corp.(70)	H
Water Res.	Harrisburg, Penn.	Data 100 Corp.(70)	H
Water Res.	Indianapolis, Indiana	Data 100 Crop.(70)	H
Water Res.	Little Rock, Arkansas	Data 100 Corp.(70)	H

Responsible Division	Location	Make (Model #)	Speed
Water Res.	Morgantown, W. Virginia	Data 100 Corp.(70)	H
Water Res.	Philadelphia, Penn.	Data 100 Corp.(70)	H
Water Res.	Sacramento, California	Data 100 Corp.(70)	H
Water Res.	Salt Lake City, Utah	Data 100 Corp.(70)	H
Water Res.	Tampa, Florida	Data 100 Corp.(70)	H
Water Res.	Trenton, New Jersey	Data 100 Corp.(70)	H
Water Res.	Boise, Idaho	IBM (1130)	H
Water Res.	Albany, New York	IBM (2780)	H
Water Res.	Takoma, Washington	IBM (2780)	H
Water Res.	Tucson, Arizona	IBM (2770)	H
Water Res.	Arlington, Virginia	Datel Corp.(30)	L
Water Res.	GSA Bldg., Wash., D.C.	IBM (2741)	L
Non-USGS Users			
Envir. Project Rev.	Int. Bldg., Wash., D.C.	Novar Corp. (5-50)	L
Library Ser.	Int. Bldg., Wash., C.C.	IBM (2780)	H
Nat. Park Ser.	1100 L St., Wash., D.C.	Datel Corp.(30)	L
Nat. Park Ser.	Atlanta, Georgia	Hetra Corp.(2)	H
Nat. Park Ser.	Denver, Colorado	Hetra Corp.(2)	H
Nat. Park Ser.	Omaha, Nebraska	Hetra Corp.(2)	H
Nat. Park Ser.	Philadelphia, Penn.	Hetra Corp.(2)	H
Nat. Park Ser.	San Francisco, California	Hetra Corp.(2)	H
Nat. Park Ser.	Santa Fe, New Mexico	Hetra Corp.(2)	H
Nat. Park Ser.	100 L St., Wash., D.C.	Hetra Corp.(2)	H
Nat. Park Ser.	Harpers Ferry, W. Virginia	Novar Corp.(5-50)	L
Nat. Park Ser.	Ohio Drive, Wash., D.C.	Novar Corp.(5—50)	L
Nat. Park Ser.	Seattle, Washington	Novar Corp.(5-50)	L
Nat. Park Ser.	1100 L. St., Wash., D.C.	Novar Corp.(5-50)	L
Nat. Park Ser.	Int. Bldg., Wash., D.C.	Novar Corp.(5-41)	L
NOAA	Whitehaven Dr., Wash., D.C.	IBM (360-20)	H
NOAA	Beaufort, North Carolina	IBM (1130)	H
NOAA	Seattle, Washington	IBM (1130)	H
Outdoor Rec.	Int. Bldg., Wash., D.C.	Novar Corp. (5-50)	L
Saline Water	Int. Bldg., Wash., D.C.	IBM (Mag. Card)	L
Sport Fisheries	Patuxent, Maryland	Novar Corp.(5-50)	L
Water Res. Research	Int. Bldg., Wash., D.C.	Datel Corp.(30)	L

All terminals are leased from vendor except New Orleans terminal.
Speed: L=Low; H=High

A4. SOME PRIVATE U.S. FIRMS PARTICULARLY ACTIVE IN THE AREA OF COMPUTER MODELING AND ANALYSIS

Anderson-Nichols
150 Causeway Street
Boston, Massachusetts 02114

Battelle, N. W.
P.O. Box 999
Richland, Washington 99352

Betz Environmental Engineers
One Plymouth Meeting Mall
Plymouth Meeting, Pennsylvania

Decision Sciences Sorporation
Benjamin Fox Pavillion
Jenkintown, Pennsylvania 19046

Engineering Science
600 Bancroft Way
Berkeley, California 94710

Environmental Dynamics, Inc.
1609 Westwood Boulevard
Suite 202
Los Angeles, California 90024

General Electric Company
3198 Chestnut Street
Philadelphia, Pennsylvania 19101

Gilbert Associates, Inc.
P.O. Box 1498
Reading, Pennsylvania 19603

Grumman Aerospace Corporation
Bethpage, New York 11714

Halcom Computer Tech.
Two Park Avenue
New York, New York 10016

Hydrocomp, Inc.
1502 Page Mill Rd.
Palo Alto, California 94304

Hydroscience, Inc.
363 Old Hook Road
Westwood, New Jersey 07675

IIT Research Institute
10 West 35th Street
Chicago, Illinois 60616

Integrated Systems
6900 Wisconsin Avenue
Chevy Chase, Maryland 20015

Lockhead Missles & Space Co.
Huntsville Research & Engineering Cen.
Huntsville Rsearch Park
4800 Bradford Drive
Huntsville, Albama 35805

Lozier Engineers, Inc.
10 Gibbs Street
Rochester, New York 14604

Metcalf & Eddy Engineers
Statler Building
Boston, Massachusetts 02116

Midwest Research Institute
425 Volker Boulevard
Kansas City, Missouri 64110

Quirk, Lawler & Matusky
415 Route 303
Tappan, New York 10983

Raytheon Company
Environmental Systems Center
Box 360
Portsmouth, Rhode Island 02871

Research Triangle Institute
Research Triangle Park
North Carolinia 27709

Roy F. Weston
Lewis Lane
West Chester, Pennsylvania 19380

Stanford Research
Menlo Park
California 94025

Storch Engineers
220 Ridgedale Ave
Florham Park, New Jersey 07932

Systems Control, Inc.
260 Sheridan Avenue
Palo Alto, California 94306

Technology, Inc.
P.O. Box 3036, Overlook Branch
Dayton, Ohio 45431

Teledyne Isotopes
50 Van Buren Avenue
Westwood, New Jersey 07675

Tetra Tech., Inc.
630 North Rosemead Boulevard
Pasadena, California 01107

TRW
One Space Park
Redondo Beach, California 90278

VTN Corporation
2301 Campus Drive
Irvine, California 92664

Wapora Inc.
1725 DeSales Street, N.W.
Washington, D.C. 20036

Water Resources Engineers, Inc.
1900 Olympic Boulevard
Walnut Creek, California 94596

A5. A SELECTED BIBLIOGRAPHY FOR ADP EQUIPMENT SELECTION AND EVALUATION PROCEDURES

ADL Systems Inc., Performance Measurement: Now you can find out what really goes on inside your computer, *Computers and Automation,* 22, 1973, 14-15.

Anderson, W.R and Sonn, E.H., How to Select a Minicomputer, *Computers and Automation,* 18, 1969, 20-22.

Arbuckle, R.A., Computer Analysis and Thruput Evaluation, *Computers and Automation,* 12, 1966, 12-16.

Blackman, M., A Specification for Computer Selection, *Data Processing,* 1973, 394-397.

Bromley, A.C., Choosing a Set of Computers, *Datamation,* 11, 1965, 37-38, 40.

Bushan, A.K., Guidelines of Minicomputer Selection, *Computer Design,* 10, 1971, 43-48.

Calingaert, P., System Performance Evaluation: Survey and Appraisal, *Communications,* ACM, 10, 1967.

Erickson, M.D. and Mahan, R.E., Process Computer System Specification, *Instruments and Control Systems,* 44, 1971.

Fife, D.W., *Alternatives in Evaluation of Computer Systems,* Mitre Corp., AD-683693, Dec. 1968.

Goff, N.S., The Case for Benchmarking, *Computers and Automation,* 22, 1973, 23-25.

Henn, R.W. and Sparr, T., Computer Selection by Water Utilities, *American Water Works Association Journal,* 61, 1969, 89-96.

Joslin, E., Cost-Value Techniques for Evaluation of Computer System Proposals, Spring Joint Computer Conference, 1964.

Joslin, E., Application Benchmark—The Key to Meaningful Computer Evaluations, *Proceedings,* ACM Conference, 1965.

Joslin, E. O. and Aiken, J.J., The Validity of Basing Computer Selections on Benchmark Results, *Computers and Automation,* 15, 1966, 22-25.

Keller, R.F. and Denham, C.R., Computer Selection Procedures, *Proceedings,* 23rd. ACM National Conference, 1968, 679-83.

McCloy, E., Some Thoughts on EDP Equipment Selection, *Journal Data Management,* 4, 1966, 20-23.

Ollivier, R.T., A Technique for Selecting Small Computers, *Datamation,* 16, 1970, 141-145.

Orlicky, J.A., Computer Selection, *Computers and Automation,* 17, 1968, 44-49.

Peebles, R., Design Considerations for a Large Computing System with a Geographically Dispersed Demand, Pennsylvania University, AD-702759, Mar. 1970.

Rosenthal, Analytic Technique for Automation Data Processing Equipment Acquisition, Spring Joint Computer Conference, 1964.

Scharf, T.G., How Not to Choose an EDP System, *Datamation,* 15, 1969, 73-74.

Schatzoff, M., Tsao, R., and Wiig, R., An Experimental Comparison of Time Sharing and Batch Processing, *Communications,* ACM, 10, 1967.

Schiffman, R.L., Report on the Special Workshop on Engineering Software Coordination, No. 72-2, University of Colorado, Boulder, Colorado, Mar. 1972.

Shinner, S.M., Which Computer; Analog, Digital, or Hybrid?, *Machine Design,* 43, 1971.

Solomon, M.B., Economics of Scale and the IBM System/360, *Communications,* ACM 10, 1966.

Weinwurm, G.F., The Description of Computer System Performance, *Proceedings,* Symposium on Economics of Automation Data Processing, Rome, October 10-22, 1965.

A6. HYDRO PROCEDURES

(adapted from Chapter III [1])

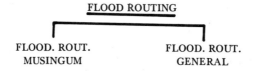

FLOOD ROUTING

FLOOD. ROUT.
MUSINGUM

FLOOD. ROUT.
GENERAL

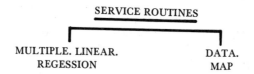

SERVICE ROUTINES

MULTIPLE. LINEAR.
REGESSION

DATA.
MAP

Program Hierarchies: Flood Routing

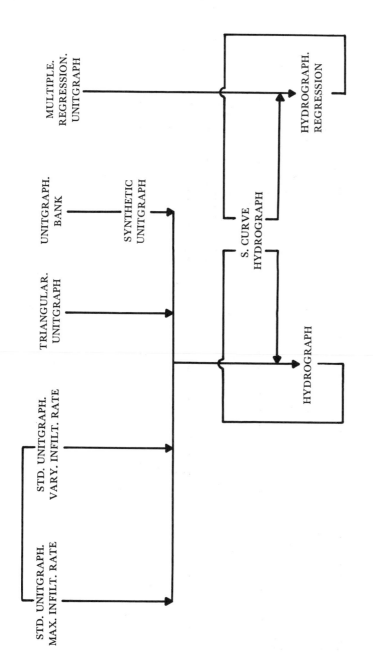

Program Hierarchies: Hydrograph Analysis

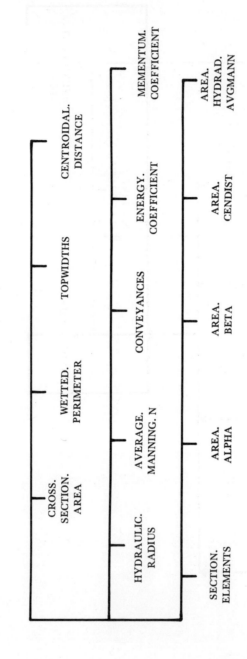

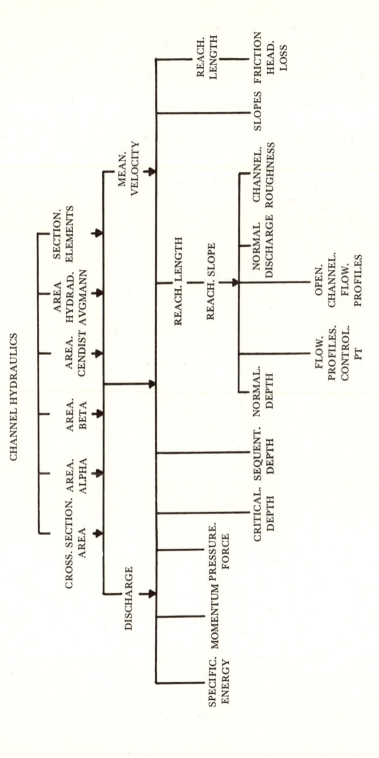

Program Hierarchies: Open Channel Hydraulics

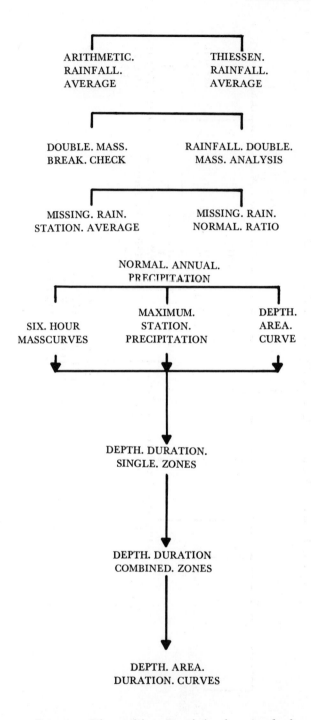

ARITHMETIC.   THIESSEN.
RAINFALL.   RAINFALL.
AVERAGE   AVERAGE

DOUBLE. MASS.   RAINFALL. DOUBLE.
BREAK. CHECK   MASS. ANALYSIS

MISSING. RAIN.   MISSING. RAIN.
STATION. AVERAGE   NORMAL. RATIO

NORMAL. ANNUAL.
PRECIPITATION

SIX. HOUR   MAXIMUM.   DEPTH.
MASSCURVES   STATION.   AREA.
                 PRECIPITATION   CURVE

DEPTH. DURATION.
SINGLE. ZONES

DEPTH. DURATION
COMBINED. ZONES

DEPTH. AREA.
DURATION. CURVES

Program Hierarchies: Precipitation Analysis

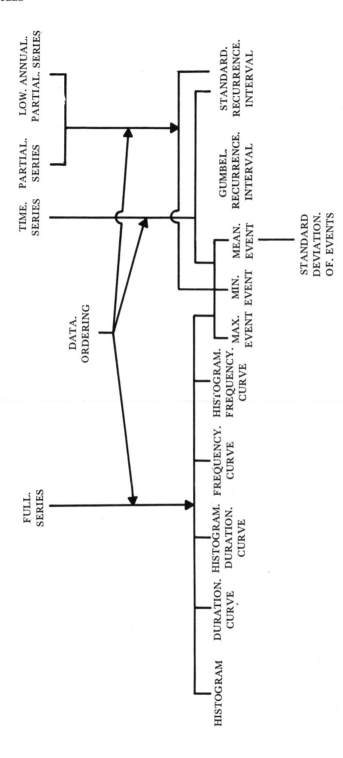

Program Hierarchies: Frequency Analysis

A7. PUBLICATIONS AVAILABLE FROM HEC
(January 1973)

HEC Annual Report
HEC Guidance Memorandum

Statistical Methods in Hydrology, Leo R. Beard (1962)

HEC Training Documents
    Water Surface Profiles (1969)
    Unit Hydrograph and Loss Rate Function (1969)
    Chemical Character of Ground Water (1970)
    Computation of Statistics for Regional Frequency Studies (1970)

HEC Research Notes
    No. 1– A Cumulus Convection Model Applied to Thunderstorm Rainfall in Arid Regions (1970)
    No. 2– An Investigation of the Determinants of Reservoir Recreation Use and Demands: The Effect of Water Surface Elevations (1972)

Methods Systemization Manuals
    Preparation of Hydrologic Engineering Computer Programs
    Reservoir Storage Yield Procedures

Proceedings of a Seminar on
    Reservoir System Analysis (November 1969)
    Sediment Transport in Rivers and Reservoirs (April 1970)
    Urban Hydrology (September 1970)
    Computer Applications in Hydrology (February 1971)
    Hydrologic Aspects of Project Planning (March 1972)

Technical Paper Series

1. Use of Interrelated Records to Simulate Streamflow
2. Optimization Techniques for Hydrologic Engineering

3. Methods for Determination of Safe Yield and Compensation Water from Storage Reservoirs
4. Functional Evaluation of a Water Resources System
5. Streamflow Synthesis for Ungaged Rivers
6. Simulation of Daily Streamflow
7. Pilot Study for Storage Requirements for Low Flow Augmentation
8. Worth of Streamflow Data for Project Design — A Pilot Study
9. Economic Evaluation of Reservoir System Accomplishments
10. Hydrologic Simulation in Water-Yield Analysis
11. Survey for Programs for Water Surface Profiles
12. Hypothetical Flood Computation for a Stream System
13. Maximum Utilization of Scarce Data in Hydrologic Design
14. Techniques for Evaluating Long-Term Reservoir Yields
15. Hydrostatistics — Principles of Application
16. A Hydrologic Water Resource System Modeling Technique
17. Hydrologic Engineering Techniques for Regional Water Resources Planning
18. Estimating Monthly Streamflows Within a Region
19. Suspended Sediment Discharge in Streams
20. Computer Determination of Flow Through Bridges
21. An Appraoch to Reservoir Temperature Analysis
22. A Finite Difference Method for Analyzing Liquid Flow in Variably Saturated Porous Media
23. Uses of Simulation in River Basin Planning
24. Hydroelectric Power Analysis in Reservoir Systems
25. Status of Water Resource Systems Analysis
26. System Relationships for Panama Canal Water Supply Study
27. Systems Analysis of the Panama Canal Water Supply
28. Digital Simulation of an Existing Water Resources System .
29. Computer Applications in Continuing Education
30. Drought Severity and Water Supply Dependability
31. Development of System Operation Rules for an Existing System by Simulation
32. Alternative Approaches to Water Resource System Simulation
33. System Simulation for Integrated Use of Hydroelectric and Thermal Power Generation

A8. BRECS PROGRAMS

The following table of contents and selected pages were adapted from the BRECS Organizational Program Index, August 1, 1972, available from U.S. Bureau of Reclamation, Denver Federal Center, Denver Colorado.

Table of Contents

Table of Contents (Cont)

ORGANIZATIONAL PROGRAM INDEX

Program title	Class	Computer/ Language	Status	Version Date	Documentation Status		
					Pro Des	User Manuals	Pro
CONCRETE DAMS SECTION							
TRANSITION GEOMETRY USING COSECANT CURVE	GEOM	CSS/BAS	0	12/71	2/72	2/72	PL
ROUTES A FLOOD THRU A RESERVOIR E/M UNITS	HYD	CSS/BAS	0	6/71	1/72	UD	U
DISCHARGE CURVE FOR DAM OUTLET WORKS	HYD	CSS/BAS	0	6/71	PL	PL	PL
SHAPE OF UPPER/LOWER NAPPE SPILLWAY CRESTS	HYD	CSS/BAS O	6/67	12/71	PL	PL	
DISCHARGE CURVE FOR DAM SPILLWAY	HYD	CSS/BAS	0	6/71	PL	PL	PL
HEAT FLOW THROUGH A MASS WITH TIME	MECH	CSS/BAS	0	11/71	1/72	1/72	PL
DIVIDES EXTERNAL LOAD FOR 2-D FINITE ELEMENT NODE	STR	CSS/BAS	0	7/71	UD	UD	UD
COMPUTE RESULTS ON ARCH DAM ABUTMENTS	STR	CSS/BAS	0	1/70	UD	UD	UD
FINITE ELEMENT ANALYSIS 2-D PROBLEMS	STR	CDC-3800/FOR	0	6/71	UD	UD	UD
SUPERPOSITION OF STRESSES	STR	CDC-3800/FOR	0	1/72	1/72	1/72	
HEAT FLOW THROUGH A MASS WITH TIME - SCHIMDT METHOD	STR	CSS/BAS	0	1/72	1/72	PL	PL
EARTH DAMS SECTION							
LISTING OF AVAILABLE SOIL AND ROCK PROPERTIES	DATA	H-800/FOR	0	1/68	PL	PL	PL
DISCHARGES THROUGH H.P. GATES AT PARTIAL OPENINGS	HYD	CSS/BAS	0	12/69	11/71	11/71	PL
COMPLEX FLOOD ROUTING PROBLEMS	HYD	CSS/BAS	0	6/67	PL	PL	PL
HYDRAULIC LOSSES IN OUTLET WORKS SYSTEMS	HYD	CSS/BAS	0	6/68	PL	PL	PL
WATER SURFACE PROFILES-CONJUGANT DEPTH	HYD	CSS/BAS	UM		PL	PL	PL
VOLUME OF OPEN CUT EXCAVATION	QUAN	CSS/BAS	0	9/71	9/71	PL	PL
PERIODIC AND CUM EARTHWORK CONTROL STATISTICS	SOIL	H-800/FOR	0	11/69	11/69*	11/69*	PL
ROLLER CURVE AND SUMMARY, CL. FREQ DIST OF BCECA	SOIL	H-800/FOR	0	6/70	6/70*	6/70*	PL
COMPUTES CONST. PORE PRESSURES IN SOIL	SOIL	CSS/BAS	0	3/69	3/69	PL	PL
BASE PRESSURE AND REINFORCEMENT FOR BASIN FLOORS	STR	CDC-3800/FOR	UM	7/71	PL	PL	PL
STRESSES IN RECTANGULAR BEAMS-WORKING STRESS DESIGN	STR	CSS/BAS	0	7/71	PL	PL	PL
MOMENT, SHEAR REINF - TOE AND HEEL FOR ARTICULATED WALLS	STR	CSS/BAS	0	7/71	3/72	PL	PL
STABILITY OF ARTICULATED WALLS AND CUTOFF DEPTH	STR	CSS6BAS	0	7/71	3/73	PL	PL
BASE PRESSURES ADD MOMENTS-BEAMS ON ELASTIC FOUNDATION	STR	CSS/FOR	0	7/71	4/72	PL	PL

Program							
HYDROLOGY BRANCH							
RAIN OR SNOW COMPUTATION OF RUNOFF	HY	H-800	0	1/66	1/66	1/66	1/66
FLOOD HYDROLOGY BRANCH							
STREAM ROUTING BY TATUMS METHOD OF SUCCESSIVE AVERAGES	HYD	H-800/FOR	0	8/65	PL	PL	PL
RESERVOIR ROUTING BY MODIFIED PULS METHOD	HYD	H-800/FOR	0	8/65	PL	PL	PL
HAZEN-TYPE FLOOD FREQUENCY ANALYSIS	HY	H-800/FOR	0	2/71	PL	PL	PL
DEPTH-DURATION ANALYSES	HY	CDC-H-800/FOR	0	8/65	PL	PL	PL
FLOOD HYDROGRAPH BY STANDARD OR DIMENSIONLESS UNITGRAPH	HY	H-800/FOR	0	7/65	PL	PL	PL
FLOOD FREQUENCY ANALYSES-PEARSON III	HY	H-800/FOR	0	2/71	PL	PL	PL
TRIANGULAR HYDROGRAPH ANALYSES	HY	H-800/FOR	0	4/70	PL	PL	PL
WATER UTILIZATION BRANCH							
EVAPOTRANSPIRATION AND IRRIGATION EFFICIENCIES	HY	CDC-H-800/FOR	UD		PL	PL	PL
CALCULATES FIELD IRRIGATION SCHEDULES	HY	H-800/FOR	UD		PL	PL	PL
MATH MODEL TO STUDY A WATER QUALITY RESOURCE SYSTEM	HY	CDC-H-800/FOR	UD		UH	UH	UH
PREDICT QUALITY CHANGES IN SOIL-WATER SYSTEM	HY	CDC-3800/FOR	UD		PL	PL	PL
FOURIER TRANSFORMS-EVALUATION OF 12 HARMONICS	NUM	CDC-3800/FOR	UD		PL	PL	PL
FIRST, SECOND, AND THIRD ORDER MARKOV CHAINS	PROB	CDC-3800/FOR	UP		PL	PL	PL
AREA-CAPACITY ANALYSIS	QUAN	CDC-3800/FOR	0	9/70	12/68	12/68	PL
AUTO CORRELATION ANALYSES	STAT	CDC-H-800/FOR	UD		PL	PL	PL
COMPUTE APPROXIMATION OF GAMMA DISTRIBUTION	STAT	CDC-3800/FOR	UD		PL	PL	PL
SORT AND MERGE BINARY-REAL AND INTEGER	SUP	CDC-3800/FOR	UD		PL	PL	PL
ALL CATHODE RAY TUBE (CRT) OUTPUTS	SUP	CDC-3800/FOR	UD		PL	PL	PL
HYDRAULICS BRANCH							
TURBINE DRAFT TUBE SURGING CHAR FROM DIMENSIONLESS DATA	HYD	H-800/FOR	0	1/69	1/72	PL	PL
TURBINE DRAFT TUBE SURGING CHAR FROM RAW DATA	HYD	H-800/FOR	0	12/70	1/72	PL	PL
DRAWDOWN CURVES WITH CURVILINEAR FLOW	HYD	H-800/FOR	0	10/68	PL	PL	PL
FLOW NET FOR ABRVT OFFSETS IN A CANAL	HYD	H-800/FOR	0	11/63	PL	PL	PL
PROTOTYPE PRESSURE COMPUTATIONS IN SLIDE GATES	HYD	H-800/FOR	0	6/64	PL	PL	PL
STREAM AND POTENTIAL FUNCT OF VORTEX IN CYLINDER	HYD	H-800/FOR	0	8/68	PL	PL	PL
REJECTION SURGES IN TRAPEZOIDAL CHANNELS	HYD	H-800/FOR	0	6/66	11/71	PL	PL
ATTENUATION OF SURGE BY A LATERAL SPILLWAY	HYD	H-800/FOR	0	11/65	11/71	PL	PL
GENERAL WATER SURFACE PROFILES BY STANDARD STEP METHOD	HYD	H-800/FOR	0	8/64	11/71	PL	PL
DISCHARGE COMPUTER FROM VELOCITY TRAVERSE IN CIRC PIPE	HYD	H-800/FOR	0	6/69	1/71	PL	PL

| Program title | Class | Computer/Language | Status | Version Date | Documentation Status | | |
					Pro Des	User (Manuals)	Pro
SELECTIVE WITHDRAWAL LAYER THICKNESS COMPUTATION	HYD	H-800/FOR	O	9/69	11/71	PL	PL
DEEP RESERVOIR TEMPERATURE PREDICTION	HYD	CDC-3800/FOR	UM		11/71	UM	UM
UNSTEADY FLOW IN TRAPEZOIDAL CHANNEL	HYD	H-800/FOR	O	12/69	1/72	PL	PL
SOLUTION OF 2D ORDER DE BY RUNGE-KUTTA MTD	NUM	H-800/FOR	O		PL	PL	PL
SIMULTANEOUS SOLN OF 2 2D ORDER DE BY RUNGE-KUTTA MTD	NUM	H-800/FOR	O		PL	PL	PL
SIMULTANEOUS SOLN OF 3 2D ORDER DE BY RUNGE-KUTTA MTD	NUM	H-800/FOR	O		PL	PL	PL
WRITES INFLOW-OUTFLOW FILE FOR TSIP	SUP	CDC-3800/FOR	O	6/70	UM	UM	UM
WRITES METEOROLOGICAL FILE FOR TSIP	SUP	CDC-3800/FOR	O	12/69	UM	UM	UM
HYDRAULICS RESEARCH SECTION							
DENSITY DETERMINATION IN A STRATIFIED FLUID	HYD	H-800/FOR	O	6/72	6/72	6/72	PL
WATER TABLE HEIGHT ABOVE PIPE DRAINS-STEADY RECHARGE	HYD	CSS/FOR		8/71	10/71	PL	PL
DRAIN SPACING-STEADY RECHARGE	HYD	CSS/FOR		8/71	10/71	PL	PL
LIGHT PATH IN STRATIFIED FLUID	HYD	H-800/FOR	O	5/72	5/72	5/72	PL
DIMENSIONLESS ADQEDUCT PARAMETERS	HYD	H-800/FOR	O	6/69	4/72	4/72	PL
ADQEDUCT SURGE CHARACTERISTICS	HYD	H-800/FOR	O	7/70	4/72	4/72	PL
SOLVES IN EQUATIONS FOR N UNKNOWNS	MAT	H-800/FOR	O	7/70	4/72	4/72	PL
ADAMS-BASHFORD NUMERICAL INTEGRATION 1ST ORDER DIFF. EQ.	NUM	H-800/FOR	O	8/71	8/71	PL	PL

CODES

O	= PROGRAM OPERATIONAL	UM	= UNDER MODIFICATION	U	= UNKNOWN
NLO	= PROGRAM NO LONGER OPERATIONAL	UD	= UNDER DEVELOPMENT	PL	= PREPARE LATER
PRO	= PROGRAM	SUB	= SUBPROGRAM	PAC	= PACKAGE
*	= DOCUMENTATION NOT IN BRECS FORMAT				

A9. GENSYS ROUTINES
(Adapted from Chapter III [29])

RC–BUILDING/1 designs and details R.C. buildings contructed from slabs, beams and columns. Conventional code of practice procedures are used for analysis and design. Calculations are taken through to the detailing of reinforcement; this has been achieved by integrating detailing programs comissioned from Messrs, W.V. Zinn & Associates, Sir Frederick Snow & Partners and Alan Marshall & Partners.

FRAME–ANALYSIS/1 analyses two or three dimensional structures composed from straight members. Many types of load, settlement or temperature effect can be applied and the engineer can select only those results which need to be examined. The subsystem was written by Messrs. Alcock, Shearing & Partners.

BRIDGE/1 analyses bridges that can be considered as continuous beams of varying sections with rigid or elastic supports. Distributed loads, point loads, settlement and temperature effects can be applied. Bending moments and shear force envelopes can be printed out as well as many other results. It was written by Messrs. Freeman Fox & Partners.

SLAB-BRIDGE/1 analyses wide bridges composed of slabs and beams of rectangular, skewed, circular or arbitrary plan form. Distributed, line, point HA and HB loads can be applied and the effect of settlement and elastic supports can also be included. Reactions, bending moments and reinforcement details can be printed out. The subsystem was written by Messrs. R. Travers Morgan & Partners.

SLIP-CIRCLE/1 is a brokered subsystem which analyses the stability of slopes using the Slip-Circle failure criterion: it incorporates the Bishop method of slices able to be varied at will by the designer. The subsystem was written by Geocomp U.K. Ltd. and has among its special features considerable flexibility in the way pore pressures may be specified. Tension cracks can be incorporated and any number of point loads can be included, acting in any direction.

INDEX

The P